Blackness and Islam

First published in February 2021 by Algorithm

Author: Dawud Walid
General Editor: AH Choudhury
Design & Typeset: Ibrahim Sadikovic

Algorithm is an imprint of Islamic Human Rights Commission Ltd,
a limited company registered in England and Wales.
Registered office: 202 Preston Road,
Wembley, Middlesex, HA9 8PA,
United Kingdom

Paperback 978-1-909853-19-5

Cover illustration: Kufic calligraphy of the *hadith*, "There is no superiority of an Arab over a non-Arab or of a non-Arab over an Arab, or of a white man over a Black man, or of a Black man over a white man, except by piety."

Blackness and Islam

Authored by
Dawud Walid

O people! Surely, We created you from a male and female and made you into nations and tribes that you may know one another. Surely the most honorable of you with Allah are those of you who have most regardfulness. Surely Allah is All-Knowing; All-Aware.

(Q.49:13)

Contents

Foreword

ANTI-BLACK racism is among the most serious challenges the American Muslim community faces. Indeed, the global *Ummah* has yet to address in a serious and thoroughgoing way the emergence of virulent forms of anti-Black racism in the past few centuries. Imam Dawud Walid has written this serious scholarly work to help address a number of grave misconceptions about how *Blackness* was understood in early Islam. In this short foreword, I want to foreground his contribution from three distinct perspectives.

Writing as a historian of Africa and Islam, I wish to offer some historical context for this important work. Writing as a practising African American Muslim I wish to offer some contemporary insight into its urgency. And finally, writing as a scholar of Islamic thought, I wish to present a timeless reminder of what is at stake.

Thinking in these distinct temporalities, I pray, will help us further establish the significance of Imam Dawud Walid's intellectual intervention.

Speaking as a historian of Africa and Islam, I must stress that it cannot be overstated just how anachronistic conceptions of *Blackness* have become in current Muslim discourses. Whether in English or Arabic, contemporary Muslim scholars often seem to believe that the contempt for Black people which has defined this five-hundred-year white supremacist era was also present in the time of the Prophet Muhammad ﷺ and his companions.

Nothing could be further from the truth. All modern concepts and constructs of skin color prejudice, whether in Western societies, Muslim societies, or any other, have been irrevocably transformed by the development of modern racial thought. And here, refracting this story through the prism of African history is crucial.

Beginning in the second half of the fifteenth century, the so-called Atlantic slave trade carried between at least twelve and twenty million sub-Saharan Africans into bondage in New World societies. We are all aware that modern racial ideologies were framed almost entirely in this period in Western societies. And we ought to call this trade by the name of its operators and beneficiaries; this was the Euro-American Slave Trade.

It was not simply Atlantic because as much as a quarter of the total volume of European slave-trading in this period took place in the Indian Ocean. Muslim societies around the Indian Ocean, especially societies of the Arabian Peninsula, began to increasingly rely on the enslavement of Black people, as did Muslim societies of the Mediterranean. The Euro-American trade had created an unprecedented mechanism for marketing human beings and racializing slavery. Whether in Christendom or the lands of Islam, this was a world awash in Black slaves.

In all these societies, whether European or Arab, Muslim or Christian, *Blackness* began to be more closely associated with low social status than ever before. The presence of race-based slavery in Arab and Persian societies emerged mainly between the seventeenth and nineteenth centuries, always as an appendage to the rise of the global capitalist commodification of Africans.

In the Western world, Old Testament texts were read in new ways to imply that Black people had always been considered inferior. In the Muslim world, prophetic traditions and classical texts were increasingly read in this way as well. In this work, Imam Dawud Walid seeks to strip away the erroneous preconceptions that have accrued, returning us to a time before modern racism, by asking a first order question of the early sources: what were the meanings ascribed to dark skin in early Islam?

Speaking as an African American Muslim, I can attest through personal experience that the lack of a self-critical consciousness of the Muslim world's recent problematic histories regarding racial slavery plays a central role in shaping race-thinking in contemporary Muslim America. Immigrant communities from Middle Eastern and South

Asian backgrounds are often coming from places with intensely racist and colorist social structures, with almost no awareness of the histories of racial slavery in those places.

Critical self-assessment of racist ideologies among many immigrant Muslim communities is in the same basic place that it was in white southern communities in the 1950s, or in Apartheid South Africa in the 1980s. Because of this, Black Muslims, whether African or African American are often subjected to the most naked possible forms of racial contempt. Racial slurs – especially '*abid*',[1] but also 'nigger' and many others – abound in American Muslim communities, and many Black Muslims are able to recount truly horrifying personal experiences of overt racial prejudice. It is as though many in these communities are unaware that it was dark-skinned Muslims – who comprised at least 10-15% of those millions of enslaved Africans – that first brought Islam to these shores.

And of course, in almost none of these communities is there any reflection on the fact that many of the characters in the Qur'an itself were Africans and/or dark-skinned people. The vast majority of the *Qasas al-Anbiya*, or Tales of the Prophets, in the Qur'an relate to stories of Black people, especially – though not exclusively – the Africans of the Nile Valley. It is worth mentioning that contemporary Africanist historical scholarship establishes unequivocally that the populations of Ancient Egypt were predominantly black and that their civilization sprang from inner African origins in the heart of the continent.

Speaking as a scholar of Islamic thought, it is worth mentioning that an important reason that people do not reflect on the 'racial identities' of Qur'anic figures is that the Qur'an is a book devoid of racial markers. There are no mentions of skin color or hair texture associated with any of the Qur'an's human characters. The only partial exception to this is – as Imam Dawud Walid reminds us – the name of the progenitor of humanity, and its first prophet. Adam's name, ﷺ, means dark brown in Arabic. With this one caveat, the Qur'an is a color-blind book.

Yet the Qur'an does offer powerful material for reflection on the problem of racism. In its telling of timeless cosmological drama, Iblis, the devil, is the first character to claim superiority on the basis of his bodily composition and his genealogical origin. This happens at the very moment when the dark-brown body of Adam ﷺ is animated (Q.38:75). In this out-of-time narrative, Iblis is cast as the primordial racist.

In this space of reflection then, racism is a spiritual sickness. It is a satanic religion that has been thrust upon humanity by an avowed enemy who hopes that we will all see one another with the same utter contempt which he has for us all. It is devilry. Nothing more, nothing less.

Imam Dawud Walid's life's work – in his previous publications, in the present volume and over the decade that I have known him – commends him as a soldier against satanic racism and especially its most perfect historical expression: white supremacy. This volume, by framing a religious response to what must be understood as a satanic spiritual attack, should be widely read and taught.

Dr. Rudolph Bilal Ware
Associate Professor of West Africa, Islamic Knowledge & Spirituality, African Diaspora at the University of California – Santa Barbara

Introduction

With the Name of Allah, the Merciful Benefactor, the Merciful Redeemer

THE PRAISE belongs to Allah ﷻ, the Sovereign, the Truth, and the Clarifier. I bear witness that there is no deity except Allah ﷻ, and I bear witness that Muhammad ﷺ is His slave-servant and His Messenger, the keeper of his promise, the trustworthy.

O Allah! Send prayers and peace upon our leader, Prophet and master Muhammad, and upon the family of our leader Muhammad, the enjoiner of good, forbidder of wrong, the fountainhead of truth and the sun of the prophetic sacred law and what follows.[2] *O Allah! Guide us with Your light to You.*[3] *Surely the best of speech is the Book of Allah [Qur'an], and the best of guidance is the guidance of Muhammad. And the worst of matters are newly invented matters [in the religion], and every newly invented matter [in the religion] is a [blameworthy] innovation.*[4] *And every [blameworthy] innovation is misguidance, and every misguidance is in the fire.*[5] We seek refuge with Allah ﷻ from misguidance and from entering into the fire.

Blackness is by no means a topic of prolific discussion within classical Islamic scholarly tradition. In comparison to subjects such as theology, jurisprudence, exegesis (*tafsir*) of the Qur'an, sciences of prophetic narrations and spiritual purification, *Blackness* and discourses on race in general would constitute a few drops in a sea of literature from the earliest centuries of Islamic history. We suggest that the issue of race was not of paramount importance to classical Islamic scholars and/or there was perhaps some intentional ignoring of the subject, which may explain why there has been only a trickle of texts written in centuries past that were solely dedicated to *Blackness* within the Muslim context.

It is understood that the first treatise to be written specifically about *Blackness* from the early Islamic period was penned by 'Amr bin Bahr al-Jahiz (may Allah have mercy upon him), a black Mu'tazili scholar from Basrah, Iraq, who lived from 159 AH to 255 AH. The treatise was controversially titled *Fakhr al-Sudan 'ala al-Bayda* (The Glory of the Blacks Over the Whites).[6] Centuries later, the Hanbali polymath Abd al-Rahman bin al-Jawzi (may Allah have mercy upon him), who lived between 510 AH to 597 AH, wrote an approximately 300 page book lauding the merits of Black people entitled *Tanwir al-Ghabash fi Fadl al-Sudan wa al-Habash* (Illuminating the Ignorant Concerning the Merit of the Blacks and the Abyssinians). The Shafi'i polymath Jalal al-Din al-Suyuti (may Allah have mercy upon him), who lived between 849 AH to 911 AH wrote three books on the topic, these being *Raf' Sha'n al-Hubshan* (Elevating the Status of the Ethiopians), *Azhar al-'Arush fi Akhbar al-Habush* (The Flowers of the Throne Concerning Information About the Ethiopians), and *Nuzhah al-'Amr fi Tafdil al-Bid wa al-Sumr* (The Promenade of Life Concerning Proclaiming the Merits for Light-Skinned, Dark-Skinned and Brown-Skinned Peoples). There were also a few additional titles written in the Arabic language from that period. In our own present century, there has been at least three books in the English language dedicated to the explicit merits of *Blackness* within Islamic discourse, two of which I co-authored, *Centering Black Narrative: Black Muslim Nobles Among the Early Pious Muslims* and *Centering Black Narrative: Ahl al-Bayt, Blackness & Africa.* The primary focus of earlier texts written in Arabic – as well as both volumes of *Centering Black Narrative* – was on *Blackness* and Black personalities within the first two to three centuries of Muslim history who resided in what is now known as the Arab world.

There were a great number of books in the early Islamic period discussing the lives of Black people. The literature included historical works written by the likes of Muhammad bin Jarir al-Tabari that chronicled the kings of Abyssinia and the Abyssinian conquest of Southern Arabia just prior to the birth of Prophet Muhammad ﷺ to chronicles of Thawrah al-Zanj (The "Negro" Revolution) which took place in Southern Iraq from 255 AH to 270 AH. The biographies of Jews, Christians, and Muslims with African heritage were also detailed in early texts. Furthermore, an ocean of books have been written about specific

civilizations and stellar personalities as well as scholarship in all of the Islamic sciences by authors who were both Black and Muslim, whose origins extended beyond the lands of the Arabs, such as in West Africa. Yet these events and biographies were not written or perceived as a genre discussing *Blackness* in meritorious isolation, like al-Jahiz and ibn al-Jawzi's aforementioned works.

Al-Suyuti wrote three separate books relating to *Blackness* as there is much to say on the topic. Similarly, I wrote this book to expand on what I have previously co-authored, due to the subject matter not being fully exhausted in the English language in those two books nor the two English translations of *Tanwir al-Ghabash.* Moreover, as the subject matter requires some additional elaboration, there were some key personalities who needed to be written about or required more elucidation from my vantage point. One noble who was intentionally omitted from *Centering Black Narrative: Black Muslim Nobles* was Bilal bin Rabah ﷺ. It was previously calculated that he should not be included as many Black Muslims feel that he is often discussed as the token or default Black Muslim when non-black Muslims speak of social egalitarianism or to prove that Islam is free of racism. I have since concluded, after discussions with contemporary Black American Muslim scholars such as Shaykh Adeynika Muhammad Mendes (may Allah preserve him) and Ustadh Rudolph Bilal Ware (may Allah preserve him) that Bilal bin Rabah's ﷺ spiritual station is too lofty to be left out of any discussion about pious Blacks from the early generations of Muslims.[7] Hence, some elements of Bilal's ﷺ stellar life will be highlighted in this book.

It is my hope that this book will help clarify and correct misconceptions about *Blackness* in Islam which have become prevalent within Muslim communities today, as well as serve as a tool in removing self-loathing among Muslims, particularly those who are Black. Moreover, it is also my hope that this work serves as a clarification of some inaccurate tropes which have been propagated by orientalists and Afrocentrists pertaining to the status of *Blackness* in the Qur'an and the authentic prophetic traditions.

May Allah ﷻ forgive me of any shortcomings, and may He forgive you and all believers. Surely, He is the Oft-Forgiving, the Merciful Redeemer.

Part One

What is Blackness?

PREMODERN Arabs understood *Blackness* very differently to how it is understood in the twenty first century in the West. Even how *Blackness* is understood among the descendants of enslaved Africans in the West today differs from how it is perceived among sub-Saharan Africans. Indeed, many dark skinned sub-Saharan Africans did not know that they were *Black* until they arrived in America. Hence, we need to clarify what *Blackness* means in the context of this book.

Africans Within *Blackness*

One group that pre-modern Arabs considered to be among the Blacks were those who they had historical contact with from the Horn of Africa. Phenotypically speaking, these Africans generally had dark brown (*al-udmah*) to black colored (*al-aswad*) skin tones with kinky (*ja'd*) hair, though not exclusively kinky. Black Africans in the generation of the Prophet Muhammad ﷺ came from the regions which constitute the contemporary areas of Ethiopia, Eritrea, Somalia, Somaliland, Djibouti, Egypt, and Sudan.

Pre-modern Arabs did not view Africa as the name of a Black continent as is popular in the modern imagination. Moreover, the Black people residing in the continent of Africa during this time did not call themselves Africans, much less have a Pan-African identity. *Ifriqiyyah* – or what could be understood as Africa back then – only included the countries that make up modern day Algeria, Tunisia, and Libya. Arabs did not become deeply acquainted with *Ifriqi* or "African" people until the conquest of *Ifriqiyyah* during the government of the third caliph

Uthman bin Affan ﷺ.[8] The predominant inhabitants of *Ifriqiyyah* were Amazigh or so-called Berber people. The Blacks which the Arabs were most familiar with in terms of socio-political interactions were the *Habashi* (Abyssinian) people and Nubians, as well as *Qibti* (Egyptian) people, many of whom looked phenotypically Nubian at that time.

Blackness, in the Arab consciousness, was expanded beyond Abyssinians/Nubians later, as Islam spread across the continent of Africa. After the first two generations of early Muslims, Zanj (which today is commonly (mis)translated as "negro") became a term for a specific type of Black people. As Zaytuna College professor Dr. Abdullah Ali pointed out, Zanj was originally used by Arabs to describe sub-Saharan Blacks who were so-called Bantu language speakers – it was not a term meant to describe all Black people.[9] Interestingly, one of the meanings of Zanj besides it being a specific group of Black people from humankind, is to have thirst (*al-atash*).[10] Besides the Zanj people, the Arabs later came into contact with others having dark brown to black skin from the Indian subcontinent and North Africa. For instance, Asma bint Abi Bakr ﷺ said, "I saw the mother of Muhammad bin al-Hanafiyyah, a black Sindi lady, who had been a slave of the tribe of Hanafiyyah."[11] Muhammad bin al-Hanafiyyah (may Allah's blessings be upon him) was one of the sons of Imam Ali bin Abi Talib ﷺ. Sindh was the location of bin Hanafiyyah's maternal lineage, and is a region in modern day Pakistan.

Arabs Within *Blackness*

Arabness and *Blackness* were not seen as mutually exclusive identities within the pre-modern Arab psyche, despite Arabs having ethnic and tribal distinctions from Abyssinians, Nubians, and Copts.

Blackness as an identity, among pre-modern Arabs, related to two factors:

1. Physical characteristics.
2. Civilizational contrast with others whom Arabs considered to be included among whiteness.

The lineage of pre-modern Arabs as well as the location of their original dwelling also provides further clarification as to why Arabs saw themselves as quasi-Blacks. As al-Jahiz stated, it was known that the Copts are originally from the Blacks, Hajar ﷺ was Coptic and her son Isma'il ﷺ is the father of the Arabs.[12] Hence the predominant skin color of pre-modern Arabs was *adam* and *al-udmah*. Ibn Manzur (may Allah have mercy upon him), who is perhaps the most famed lexicologist of the Arabic language, stated in this regard that *adam* in the context of color meant brown, and *al-udmah*, which is linguistically related to *adam*, meant dark brown, as it relates to descriptors for people.[13] Banu Sulaym, an Arab tribe from the Hijaz portion of Arabia, was known, for instance, for its members having black skin.[14] Regarding hair texture of the Arabs of old, al-Zamakhshari stated, "It is dominant among the Arabs to have kinky hair."[15]

The manifestation of *Blackness* within pre-modern Arab communities is also understood through a well-known prophetic narration relating to recessive genes. As narrated by Abu Hurayrah ﷺ in an authentic tradition, a man came to the Prophet ﷺ and exclaimed,

> "O Messenger of Allah! My wife gave birth to a black boy." The Prophet replied, "Do you have camels?" The man replied, "Yes." He then asked, "What color are they?" The man responded, "Red." He then inquired, "Are any of them grey?" The man responded, "Yes." He then asked, "Where do you think these colors came from?" The man replied, "It is from hereditary disposition." He then told him, "Surely, your son is from the hereditary disposition [of his ancestors]."[16]

As the Prophet Muhammad ﷺ was an Arab, *Blackness* was in his lineage as well as in his progeny, including close descendants who were described as having kinky hair and/or dark to black skin color. According to al-Jahiz, ten of the sons of Abd al-Muttalib, the paternal grandfather of Prophet Muhammad ﷺ, were *dulm* meaning extremely dark.[17] Imam Muhammad al-Baqir bin Ali bin Husayn bin Ali bin Abi

Talib (may Allah's blessings be upon them) was described as having kinky hair and brown skin.[18] His son Imam Ja'far al-Sadiq (may Allah's blessings be upon him), who was described as light brown, also had kinky hair.[19] Imam Muhammad al-Nafs al-Zakiyyah bin Abdillah bin Hasan bin Hasan bin Ali bin Abi Talib (may Allah's blessings be upon them) was described as being black in skin color, the same skin tone as the famed Abyssinian companion Bilal bin Rabah ﵁.[20] In emphasis of this point, ibn al-Rumi (may Allah have mercy upon him) in a line of poetry directed towards Ja'far al-Mutawakkil – an Abbasid ruler who was hostile towards the descendants of Fatima al-Zahra ﵂ – remarked:

> You insult [the progeny of Prophet Muhammad] due to their Blackness while they are pure Arabs with dark complexion.
>
> However, you are blue [eyed] – the Roman people have embellished your faces with their color.[21]

Even the term *sayyid* which carries the meaning of one who is a descendant of Prophet Muhammad ﷺ – usually from the offspring of Imam Husayn bin Ali ﵁ – has a linguistic relationship to *aswad/sud* meaning black/blacks. Hence in the Imami Shi'ah tradition, the *sayyid* who is a religious scholar wears a black turban while the scholar who is not a sayyid wears a white turban. *Blackness*, therefore, has a connection in the Arabic language to mastery, similar to how in martial arts the black belt represents the highest level of mastery over brown, yellow, and white belts, not that black skin of humans is superior over brown, yellow, or white skin tones. A linguistic example of this can be seen in the statement of Umar bin al-Khattab ﵁, "Obtain deep understanding before ruling" – ruling or governing people in this statement (*tusawwadu*) is etymologically connected to *aswad*.[22]

Further, Arabs should not be viewed as a homogenous race nor as a Mediterranean sub-race within the false constructs of Eurocentric taxonomy and anthropology. Arabness is not a genetic race per se. Arabness has classically been defined as those who have paternal lineage from Arabs and/or normative cultural connection with Arabs

which is primarily manifested by speaking Arabic. Therefore, we see in pre-modern Arab societies that individuals with non-Arab maternal lineage were considered as Arabs within their tribes. From Quraysh, Umar bin al-Khattab's paternal great-grandmother and grandmother were Abyssinians.[23] His strong connection to Abyssinian blood, however, did not exclude him from being an Arab noble who would later ascend to be the caliph. As mentioned previously, Muhammad bin al-Hanafiyyah, one of the sons of Ali bin Abi Talib, was a Hashemite although his mother was South Asian. Zayd bin Hasan bin Zayd bin Hasan bin Ali bin Abi Talib (may Allah's blessings be upon them) too was a Hashemite who had a Nubian mother.[24] Likewise, Imam Muhammad al-Jawad bin Ali al-Rida bin Musa al-Kazim bin Ja'far al-Sadiq (may Allah's blessings be upon them) was a Hashemite who had a Nubian mother.[25] Imam al-Jawad's mother reportedly "was a Nubian from the people of the household of Mariyah al-Qibtiyyah, the mother of Ibrahim the son of the Messenger of Allah".[26] Idris bin Musa bin Abdillah bin Musa bin Abdillah bin Hasan bin Hasan bin Ali bin Abi Talib (may Allah's blessings be upon them), an ancestor of Abd al-Qadir al-Jiylani (may Allah have mercy upon him), had an Amazighi mother.[27] There are also several dozen other notable men and women among the pre-modern Arabs from Quraysh as well as its sub-clan of the Hashemites who had full status as Arab nobles while having mothers from the lands of non-Arab Blacks. This is quite different from the (white) American construct of race which permeates Western societies today; that having white paternal lineage and Black maternal ancestry automatically posits one as outside of white socio-political designation, both explicitly and implicitly.

Pre-modern Arabs also viewed *Blackness* as being in contrast to foreign civilizations; there are prophetic narrations which point toward this reality. One example of this meaning relates to the companion Abdullah bin Mas'ud's desire for his sister to be married, saying that he called out to Allah for her to marry a Muslim "even if he is an *ahmar* Roman or a Black Abyssinian".[28] Another example is the well-known *hadith* narrated by Muslim and Ahmad bin Hanbal which stated, "I was sent to the *ahmar* and the Black." As the *hadith* commentator al-Nawawi (may Allah have mercy upon him) stated relating to this *hadith*,

one of the meanings of *ahmar*, which literally means red, is the non-Arab white people.[29] Ibn Manzur stated the same in referencing the same *hadith* as it refers to *ahmar*.[30] By non-Arab peoples, they were referring to the Romans and the Persians. Al-Jahiz stated about this narration, "For we are the true Blacks whereas the Arabs are most resembling the pure Blacks [meaning Arabs are quasi-Blacks]."[31] Ibn al-Shajari (may Allah have mercy upon him) stated in the context of this *hadith* that the Arabs understood red people to mean white people.[32] Likewise, al-Sahib bin Abbad (may Allah have mercy upon him) stated that those who are red meant non-Arabs.[33] So, within the pre-modern Arab mindset, whites were societal foreigners who were the opposite of themselves. Therefore, due to lineage, melanin content and cultural interactions, pre-modern Arabs saw themselves as being more aligned with and connected to *Blackness* than whiteness.

In another narration – which is less popular although considered to be authentic by al-Haythami – al-Hakim narrated there is a clear indication pointing to the relationship between *Blackness* and Arabness. In a dream related to Abu Bakr ﵁, the Prophet ﷺ stated,

> "I had a dream of myself being followed by black sheep that were being followed by white sheep until the black sheep could no longer be seen." Abu Bakr replied, "O Messenger of Allah! As for the black sheep, they are the Arab. The white sheep are the non-Arab. They will enter Islam until the Arabs will no longer be recognized due to their numerousness." The Prophet replied, "This is the exact interpretation given to me by an angel prior to the dawn."[34]

This *hadith* has manifested into contemporary reality as centuries of Arab men have sired children by lighter skinned non-Arab women through marriage and concubinage, producing millions of Arabs who phenotypically today bear lesser resemblance to pre-modern Arabs. This phenomenon, as mentioned previously in the quote of ibn al-Rumi, began during the time of the Abbasid dynasty. As al-Jahiz commented, during this era, although the men of Basrah in Iraq desired women from

the Indian subcontinent while the men of Yemen desired Abyssinian ladies, men from Greater Syria had the greatest attraction for Romans – meaning white women.[35]

As it relates to the term *abyad*, which literally means white, this term carried more than one meaning for pre-modern Arabs, though this is commonly misunderstood by contemporary Arabic speakers who understand this term literally when applied to skin color. In the most literal sense, white skin as a non-pejorative description for Arabs of old meant resembling the color of wheat, given they overwhelmingly did not look like Romans that possessed less melanin.[36] Ibn Manzur further elaborated that white skin for Arabs at that time not only meant the color of wheat but also light brown.[37] Arabs would describe a person as white to praise their inward nobility or character or state the person is free of blemishes; this is what was meant by a man or woman having a "white face".[38] Sharif al-Murtada wrote about whiteness as it related to people, "it is the handsomeness of the people regarding reputation and their nobility as it relates to their character."[39]

To summarize, the pre-modern Arabs did not equate Africa with *Blackness,* in fact their notion of Africa was limited to areas covered by modern day Libya, Algeria and Tunisia. Furthermore, Arabness was associated with being Black, or at least seen as a derivative of *Blackness*. Finally, Arabs who were considered as Black (because of their skin color or maternal ancestry) were not marginalized for their *Blackness*.

Black Figures in the Qur'an

THE QUR'AN does not explicitly mention the skin tones of prophets, saints, and transgressors within it. Moreover, it is silent on stating that such and such nations were from the Blacks and such and such tribes were from the whites. Allah ﷻ is specific in saying, however, "*And certainly We sent to every nation a messenger…*" (Q.16:36) Hence every nation of people was sent a prophet to serve as a bringer of glad tidings and as a warner. This includes Blacks and whites, Arabs and non-Arabs.

As the Qur'an is a colorblind book – in the sense that it is silent on mentioning skin colors of the characters discussed – there are hints as to the colors of some, as well as descriptions from the Prophet ﷺ and the early generations of Muslims about certain personalities' physical traits. The one prophet for whom there is a strong indication of his being dark in color is Adam ﷺ. As mentioned previously, *adam* as a color of a person in classical Arabic means brown, like topsoil from the earth.[40] Regarding the creation of Adam ﷺ, the Qur'an states, "*And indeed, We created man from dried clay of stinky mud.*" (Q.15:26) According to al-Razi, the word for mud (*al-hama*) in this verse means dirt which is black in color.[41] But Allah ﷻ knows best the actual skin color of Adam ﷺ.

There are five persons mentioned by name in the Qur'an who can be reasonably presumed to have been phenotypically Black through their physical descriptions given by the Prophet ﷺ and the early righteous Muslims.

Musa ﷺ

The Messenger of Allah ﷺ stated that "I saw Musa, he had black skin".[42] Another prophetic narration said that he had "brown skin and kinky hair".[43] Yet another narration stated that during the Night Journey,[44] the Prophet ﷺ saw Musa ﷺ and described him as dark skinned and tall, like the men from the tribe of Shanwa, which is one of the early tribes of Arabs from Yemen.[45]

Relating to one of the miracles of Musa ﷺ, the Qur'an mentions, "*And he drew forth his hand then it was white to those who saw.*" (Q.7:108) In explanation of this verse several scholars of *tafsir* including al-Tabari, al-Qurtubi, al-Baghawi and al-Baydawi mentioned that Musa ﷺ was dark in skin color. Obviously if Musa's ﷺ hand was already white, it would not have been a miracle when he pulled it out from his chest that it appeared the same color.

It is worth noting that the ancient Egyptians were also Black. Hence, it can be reasonably deduced that Pharaoh, the archetype of tyranny mentioned in the Qur'an, was Black as well as his pious wife Asiya ﷺ, who the Prophet ﷺ mentioned as one of the four most virtuous believing women.[46]

Luqman ﷺ

The Prophet ﷺ said, "Take from the Blacks, for surely there are three from among them that are from the leaders of the people of paradise: Luqman the Wise, al-Najashi, and Bilal the Prayer-caller."[47] Al-Tabarani stated that Blacks here means Abyssinians. In another narration, it is stated, "The leaders of the Blacks are four: Luqman the Abyssinian, al-Najashi, Bilal, and Mihja'."[48] Sa'id bin al-Musayyab said that Luqman ﷺ was a Black man from the Blacks of Egypt possessing esoteric knowledge, Allah ﷻ gave him wisdom but not prophethood,[49] this was said in explanation of a verse in the chapter of the Qur'an named after Luqman ﷺ which says, "*And certainly We gave Luqman wisdom.*" (Q.31:12)

Allah ﷻ relays the following words of wisdom from Luqman ﷺ:

> *When Luqman said to his son, counselling him, "My son, do not associate anything with Allah. Associating others with Him is a terrible wrong."* (Q.31:13)
>
> *[And Luqman said], "My son, even if something weighs as little as a mustard-seed and is within a rock or anywhere in the heavens or in the earth, Allah will bring it out. Indeed, Allah is Subtle and Acquainted.*
>
> *My son, establish the prayer, and command what is right and forbid what is wrong, and be steadfast in the face of all that happens to you. That is certainly the most resolute course to follow.*
>
> *Do not avert your face from people out of haughtiness and do not strut about arrogantly on the earth. Allah does not love anyone who is vain or boastful.*
>
> *Be moderate in your tread and lower your voice. The most hateful of voices is the donkey's bray."* (Q.31:16-19)

Some of his wise statements include:

> Surely when Allah ﷻ praises a thing, He protects it.[50]
>
> O my son! Increase the prayer 'My Lord, forgive me'. Surely to Allah ﷻ there is an hour in which He does not refuse the asker.[51]
>
> An adversary with forbearance is better than a foolish friend.[52]

The Companions of Al-Ukhdud

Allah ﷻ states:

The companions of al-Ukhdud (the ditch) were killed
The fire possessing fuel
When they sat by it
And witnessed what they were doing against the believers
They had nothing against them except that they believed in
Allah, the Mighty, Praiseworthy. (Q.85:4-8)

Imam Ali bin Abi Talib ؓ said that the prophet sent to the companions of al-Ukhdud was Abyssinian, those who believed in him and warned their king against immorality were burned alive in a ditch.[53]

Dhul Qarnayn ؑ

The Qur'an stated, "*And they ask you [O Prophet] regarding Dhul Qarnayn. Say! 'I will recite to you about him a report.'*" (Q.18:83) Imam Ali bin Abi Talib ؓ said of him that "Dhul Qarnayn was a Black man".[54] Imam Ali ؓ also stated that he was a righteous slave from the first generations of the children of Japheth, the son of Nuh ؑ.[55] Another report relayed by ibn al-Jawzi stated that Dhul Qarnayn ؑ passed away during the lifetime of Ibrahim ؑ, and Allah ﷻ knows best.[56]

Isa ؑ

It is narrated that the Prophet ﷺ saw in a dream two men making *tawaf* around the Ka'bah, one of them was *adam* in skin color and the other was white. The one who was *adam* in skin color was the son of Maryam ؑ while the one who was white was the *Dajjal* (false messiah).[57] It has also been described by commentators that Isa's ؑ skin color was between reddish to dark brown meaning light brown, but Allah ﷻ knows best.

Zayd bin Harithah ﷺ

Zayd bin Harithah ﷺ is the only one of the Prophet's ﷺ companions mentioned by name in the Qur'an. His mention is related to Zaynab bint Jahsh ﷺ , one of the Mothers of the Believers, who Zayd ﷺ had been married to, but after they divorced she married the Prophet ﷺ. The adversaries of the Prophet ﷺ ridiculed him for this marriage because he raised Zayd ﷺ like a son after emancipating him from slavery. Allah ﷻ then revealed:

> *And remember [O Prophet] when you said to the one on whom Allah bestowed favor 'Keep your wife and be regardful of Allah' while you concealed within yourself that which Allah is to disclose. And you feared people while Allah has more right that you fear Him. So, when Zayd had no longer any need for her, We married her to you in order that there not be upon the believers any discomfort concerning the wives of their foster guardianship when they no longer have need of them. And ever is the command of Allah accomplished.* (Q.33:37)

Zayd ﷺ, who was an Arab, was described as short with intensely dark skin and was flat-nosed.[58]

Part Two

Clarifying Problematic Narrations & Verdicts Relating to Blackness

ORIENTALISTS – including Black orientalists, from the twentieth century until today – critique Islam by pointing to certain Muslim texts which they say is evidence that Islam is inherently anti-Black. Some have gone to the extent of telling Black people who have embraced Islam that they have traded in the religion of the racist slave-master, meaning (white) Christianity, for the religion of another racist, referring to (Arab) Islam.

There have always been tribalistic and racist Muslims going back to the earliest generations. Over time the Muslim world saw influences that are foreign to the authentic teachings of the Prophet ﷺ creep into Muslim scholarly literature. Moreover, there are religious opinions which were issued by pious yet fallible men, which when read in our contemporary context appear to be racist against Black people. To fully understand why such texts, influences and opinions found their way into Muslim discourse, we need to examine and understand three issues: the influences of *Isra'iliyyat* within texts written by Muslim scholars; narrations which were fabricated in the name of the Prophet ﷺ; and misinterpreted narrations and erroneous religious opinions issued by early scholars about the "negro".

Jewish Lore (*Isra'iliyyat*) Within Muslim Texts

One category of texts which are viewed as anti-Black are what are termed as *Isra'iliyyat*. These texts are not found in the Qur'an nor can they be correctly attributed to the Prophet Muhammad ﷺ. *Isra'iliyyat* are biblical and other folk tales that early Muslims heard from the People of the Book (Christians and Jews) which were later unintentionally woven into texts written or compiled by Muslims as *hadiths* or statements of early Muslims. There were a number of reasons why *Isra'iliyyat* entered into Muslim discourses which then found their way into Muslim books. The most generous explanation, and most likely of these reasons, is that the Qur'an and the Prophet ﷺ relate numerous stories about the prophets sent to the Children of Israel. Oftentimes these stories are succinct and seek to impart a moral message. They did not mention by name a number of the prophets sent to the Children of Israel and also left out many details about a number of them, though their names were known by Muslims. This lack of detail in the Qur'an and prophetic narrations led some early Muslims to turn to the *Isra'iliyyat* as a way of filling in the informational gaps.[59] In this process of learning from *Isra'iliyyat,* some early Muslims, innocently and mistakenly, ascribed many stories to the Prophet ﷺ and other early Muslims, which were in fact Jewish lore. Al-Dhahabi took another view, that certain stories were fabricated intentionally and passed on to Muslims by those who were adversaries of Islam.[60]

Before touching on the issue of anti-Blackness as it relates to *Isra'iliyyat,* we will look at how Jewish stories crept into Islamic texts and even influenced the theology of some Muslims.

The Hadith of the Slave Girl

There is a suspect *hadith* which purports that a man came to the Messenger of Allah ﷺ with a non-Arab slave woman who accepted Islam. The Messenger of Allah ﷺ then allegedly questioned her by saying, "Where is Allah?" She then reportedly pointed up to the sky. Then he asked, "Who am I?" She then supposedly pointed to the

Messenger of Allah ﷺ, then to the sky, so he said, "Free her; she is a believer."[61] Al-Mizzi graded a narrator within the chain to be weak, and weak narrations are not to be used as theological proofs.[62] Beyond the issue of the chain of narration, the *hadith* contradicts the Qur'an and reflects anthropomorphism which is common place in Jewish tales. Sayyid Hasan al-Saqqaf (may Allah have mercy upon him) argues that anthromorphism in *hadith* literatue comes from *Isra'iliyyat* and stated that this particular narration with this wording is a solitary report (*hadith ahad*) which lacks basis as a theological proof.[63] The Qur'an clearly states, *"He [Allah] is not like anything."* (Q.42:11) In relation to the prophetic prayer, "You are Evident and not physically above anything, and You are the Hidden and not physically beneath anything," al-Bayhaqi stated that Allah ﷻ not being physically above nor beneath anything means that He is not in a location.[64] This means that Allah ﷻ is not up in the sky nor on earth as the Jewish people have relayed that "They heard the sound of the Lord God walking in the garden in the cool of the day." (Genesis 3:8)

In contrast, another version of the same event in a prophetic narration which is not mixed with *Isra'iliyyat* anthropomorphism is that a man from the Ansar along with a Black slave woman came to the Prophet ﷺ who said to the man, "If you see that she is a believer, free her." Then the Prophet ﷺ asked her, "Do you testify that there is no deity except Allah?" She replied, "Yes." He then inquired, "Do you testify that Muhammad is the Messenger of Allah?" She said, "Yes." He then asked, "Do you believe in the resurrection [after physical death]?" She replied, "Yes." He ﷺ then said, "Free her." This *hadith* is authentic.[65]

Curse of Ham

The most infamous example of anti-Black *Isra'iliyyat* is of the cursed offspring of Ham bin Nuh, which has made its way into texts of Sunni and Shi'i Muslims alike. The Bible relayed:

> *These are the three sons of Noah: and of them was the whole earth overspread.*

> *And Noah began to be a husbandman, and he planted a vineyard:*
> *And he drank of the wine, and was drunken; and he was uncovered within his tent.*
> *And Ham, the father of Canaan, saw the nakedness of his father, and told his two brethren without.*
> *And Shem and Japheth took a garment, and laid it upon both their shoulders, and went backward, and covered the nakedness of their father; and their faces were backward, and they saw not their father's nakedness.*
> *And Noah awoke from his wine, and knew what his younger son had done unto him.*
> *And he said, Cursed be Canaan; a servant of servants shall he be unto his brethren.*
> *And he said, Blessed be the Lord God of Shem; and Canaan shall be his servant.* (Genesis 9:19-26)

The Babylonian Talmud – which is a collection of sayings of Jewish rabbis and sages – states:

> *Our Rabbis taught: Three copulated in the ark, and they were all punished – the dog, the raven, and Ham. The dog was doomed to be tied, the raven expectorates [his seed into his mate's mouth] and Ham was smitten in his skin.*[66]

In both narratives, Nuh ﷺ supposedly cursed Ham's offspring which made one of Ham's son's subservient and this was reflected in their being made Black.

Within Muslim texts there are three different accounts of Nuh ﷺ and his son Ham which mirror the Jewish tales, minus Nuh ﷺ getting drunk.

The first account includes a narration attributed to Imam Ali al-Hadi (may Allah's blessings be upon him) wherein it is stated that a wind blew the garment off of Nuh's ﷺ private parts as a result of which his two sons, Ham and Japheth, laughed at him. This allegedly caused Nuh ﷺ to raise his hands to the sky and pray to Allah ﷻ to change the semen of

the loins of Ham so that his progeny would be Black and that Japheth's would give birth to the Turks from whom Ya'juj and Ma'juj would come, as well as the people of China.[67] The Imami Shi'i historian al-Ya'qubi narrated a similar version without mentioning the name of Imam al-Hadi as the narrator, though he mentions that from the cursed offspring of Ham came the Copts, Abyssinians, and the people of Hind meaning South Asians. He also narrates that they would obey Satan in sport and also play in falsehood.[68]

The second version is narrated by Sunni scholar al-Quda'i, who mentions that Ham's offspring were turned Black while Japheth was exonerated from being cursed by the prayer of Nuh.[69]

In another version, Al-Tabari repeated the Talmudic portion that Ham had intercourse with a woman in the ark which prompted Nuh to curse him, causing his sperm to produce Black people.[70]

In addressing the problematic aspects of these narratives, the first issue to focus on in the original Jewish tale is that of Nuh reportedly being drunk due to alcohol consumption. Islamic theologians robustly reject this claim, that Nuh, or for that matter any prophet, got inebriated from intoxicants. This claim is in fact considered to be slander against Nuh; thus, the occasion that gave rise to him cursing the offspring of Ham is deemed to be false which leads to the impossibility of the curse itself. As stated by Ustadh Abd al-Qahir bin Tahir al-Tamimi al-Baghdadi, it is the consensus of Islamic scholars that it is a necessity that all prophets are protected (*ma'sumun*) after prophethood from all sins (*dhunub*), and that lapses in memory or innocent mistakes are not sins (a mistake is other than intentional and prophets are protected from committing intentional errors).[71] Thus Isa did not make it permissible to eat pork, for surely eating pork is forbidden in every sacred law given to prophets; and likewise he did not actually say that partaking in a little bit of wine makes the heart happy.[72]

Thus, Adam approaching the tree which he was commanded to stay away from was out of forgetfulness, not intentional disobedience, as Allah said, "*And most certainly We made a covenant with Adam from before, but he forgot.*" (Q.20:115) Likewise, Nuh did not take wine on the ark to begin with. To have taken wine on the ark to drink would not have been a lapse of memory but a premeditated act. Messengers and

prophets did not prohibit for their families and followers the consumption of alcohol to then hypocritically consume it themselves. Allah ﷻ rhetorically asked those who claimed to follow the prophets, *"Do you enjoin righteousness for people and forget it yourselves yet you recite the Scripture? Do you not have intelligence?"* (Q.2:44) Thus prophets such as Nuh ﷺ did not engage in committing major sins, for common people would have used as excuses with Allah ﷻ that they could not believe in men who claimed to be divinely guided yet openly practised hypocrisy. Therefore, it is theologically impossible in traditional Islam to accept that Nuh ﷺ got intoxicated as a result of which he got angry and cursed his son.

The narration which claimed that Imam Ali al-Hadi stated that Nuh ﷺ prayed against his son which caused his offspring to turn Black, and others similar to it, are considered non-authoritative and unsound according to ibn al-Jawzi.[73]

Beyond the issue of mistakes or weaknesses in the chains of narration, another theological issue arises, which is the slander that Nuh ﷺ would pray for his innocent unborn grandchildren and their offspring to be cursed. Allah ﷻ said, *"We sent Our messengers with clear signs, and sent down with them the Book and the balance in order to establish justice among people."* (Q.57:25) Allah ﷻ also stated, *"And no bearer of burdens shall bear another's."* (Q.35:18) It would have been unjust for Nuh ﷺ to have cursed his own grandchildren and generations to come for the reported sin of his son laughing at his nakedness. Nuh ﷺ was a steadfast messenger with the highest ethical conduct who would have never prayed against any innocent life, much less his own progeny.[74]

The third theological discrepancy with this folklore is its contradiction with the Qur'an, which asserts that no ethnic group has inherent superiority over another. Allah ﷻ clearly stated,

> *O people! Surely, We created you from a male and female and made you into nations and tribes that you may know one another. Surely the most honorable of you with Allah are those of you who have most regardfulness. Surely Allah is All-Knowing; All-Aware.* (Q.49:13)

In further emphasis of this, the Prophet ﷺ stated:

> O people! Surely your Lord is one, and surely your father is one. Surely there is no virtue of the Arab over the non-Arab, nor the non-Arab over the Arab, nor the Black over the white, nor the white over the Black except in regardfulness (*taqwa*).[75]

Mujahid bin Jabr (may Allah have mercy upon him), who was Black and a student of Abdullah ibn Abbas ﷺ, said in commentary of Q.49:13 that nations means distant lineages while tribes means closer to those in lineage. Sa'id ibn Jubayr (may Allah have mercy upon him), who was also Black and a student of Abdullah ibn Abbas ﷺ, concurred that nations means lineage.[76] Hence, the Qur'an makes clear that there is nothing inherently inferior relating to lineage, meaning that the offspring of Ham and Japheth possess general spiritual and moral equality with the offspring of Shem. This understanding of the Qur'an refutes the idea found in the *Isra'iliyyat* that certain ethnic groups are intrinsically inferior to others and thus deserving of enslavement.

On Adam ﷺ Desiring to be White

Another *Isra'iliyyat* which found its way into a famed text among Muslims is the tale that Adam ﷺ received heavenly advice about how to become literally white in skin color. *Al-Ghunyah li Talibi Tariq al-Haqq wa al-Din* by the renowned Hanbali scholar Abd al-Qadir al-Jiylani has a narration attributed to Imam Ali bin Abi Talib ﷺ stating:

> Antarah said that he asked Ali, 'Why do you call these the white days?'
>
> Ali replied, "when Allah, the Most High, brought Adam from paradise to earth, the sun scorched him, thus his body become Black. Then Jibril came to him and said, 'O Adam! Would you not love that your

> body be made white?' Adam replied, 'Yes.' Jibril then told him, 'Then fast in every month the thirteenth, fourteenth, and fifteenth days.' So, Adam fasted the first of these days and became slightly white, then fasted the second day and became whiter, then fasted the third day and his entire body turned white. And this is how these days were named the white days.[77]

Al-Jiylani then states, "Thus Adam is from those for whom fasting was prescribed before [Prophet] Muhammad." This statement, which was repeated by al-Suhrawardi without attribution to Imam Ali ﷺ, implies that Allah ﷻ prescribed the first fast for humans upon the first prophet, the reward of which was white skin color.[78]

Regarding this saying attributed to Imam Ali ﷺ, there is no chain of narration which connects him to this speech. He is the man about whom the Prophet ﷺ stated, "I am the house of wisdom, and Ali is its door."[79] Sidi Ahmad al-Tijani (may Allah have mercy upon him) said of him that he is the gate to the house of prophetic knowledge, not anyone else from among the other caliphs and companions.[80] Besides there being no chain of narration for this saying attributed to Imam Ali ﷺ, it is inconceivable that he would give such an explanation as it relates to Adam's ﷺ *Blackness,* since it contradicts the Qur'an and several soundly narrated prophetic teachings that there is no virtue of any particular skin color over others. Moreover, the term used for Black in this narration (*aswad*) in relation to Adam's ﷺ body cannot be taken metaphorically as it is in the verse which discusses those who die with defective faith and character: *"On the day of Judgment, those who lied against Allah their faces will be made black (muswaddah)."* (Q.39:60) This is because the forms of the nouns carry different meanings; *aswad* is used in a literal sense in the saying attributed to Imam Ali, while *muswaddah* in the Qur'anic context of blacken faces is metaphorical.

This false attribution to Imam Ali ﷺ is clearly in the same category of *Isra'iliyyat* tales fabricated about Nuh ﷺ which stems from the Book of Genesis in the Hebrew Bible.

Anti-Black Sayings Falsely Relayed in the Name of the Prophet ﷺ

Just as there are apocryphal Jewish tales which were repeated in Muslim texts, there are many fabricated *ahadith* that were relayed in the name of the Prophet Muhammad ﷺ. These fabrications range from statements that have serious theological ramifications, if unwittingly accepted, to those which may seem more benign. These fabricated *ahadith* include anti-Black narrations relating to a specific group of Black people, the Zanj, not all Blacks.

Anti-Zanj Narrations

One narration which stigmatizes the Zanj is a narration in which the Prophet ﷺ supposedly prohibited the eating of meat slaughtered by the Zanj in their land. This narration was graded by ibn Hibban to be a strongly reprehensible narration.[81] Another such narration, which was also denounced by ibn Hajar al-'Asqalani to be a lie, is that the Prophet ﷺ also banned the eating of meat slaughtered by the jinn and the Zanj.[82] In Islamic law, other than out of dire necessity, it is impermissible for Muslims to eat the meat of pagans, assuming that Zanj equaled pagans in this period. Leaving aside the weaknesses in the chains of these problematic narrations, they do not mention pagans in general but focus on a specific people, the Zanj. It would be equally impermissible to eat the meat of pagans from other jurisdictions outside of the lands of the Zanj. Many men and women from among the Zanj became Muslims within the early generations of Muslims. It is of course permissible for Muslims to eat the meat of other Muslims, including Muslims from the Zanj people. Furthermore, it is unclear how general Muslims would knowingly eat the meat of jinn, even if the latter dubious narration was considered acceptable.

Another anti-Black saying fabricated in the *hadith*, "Beware of marriage to the Zanj, for surely they are disfigured people."[83] This *hadith* is found in *Usul al-Kafi* by the Imami Shi'i *hadith* scholar al-Kulayni and was declared to be fabricated by *hadith* critics. Ibn Hibban had declared it to be a complete fabrication.[84] The prolific Maliki scholar, ibn Abd al-

Barr (may Allah have mercy upon him), also declared it to be reprehensibly bogus with no foundation to it.[85] Ibn al-Jawzi stated that it was completely false and unfounded.[86] Though Zanj speaks to a particular group of Black people, there is no such authentic admonishment by the Prophet ﷺ banning Arabs from marrying the Zanj or any other African people. This issue was clarified by Imam Zayd bin Ali bin Husayn (may Allah's blessings be upon them), one of the Prophet's ﷺ descendants and a teacher of Abu Hanifah (may Allah have mercy upon him), when he pointed out the following:

> People are compatible for one another from among Arabs, non-Arabs, those from Quraysh and from the Hashemites, when they enter into Islam and believe; their *deen* is one... Certainly, Zayd bin Harithah, a former slave, married Zaynab bint Jahsh, a lady from Quraysh. Bilal married Halah bint Awf, the sister of Abdur Rahman bin Awf [who was one of the richest of the Sahabah]. Zurayq, a man freed from slavery by the Messenger of Allah, married Amrah bint Bishr bin Abi Al-Aws bin Umayyah. Abdullah bin Razah, a man freed from slavery by Mu'awiyah, married bint 'Amr bin Hurayth. Ammar bin Yasir married the sister of 'Amr bin Hurayth. Abu Mijdham bin Abi Fakihah married a lady from Bani Zuhrah.[87]

The Prophet ﷺ himself arranged and conducted marriages of whites with Blacks.

Yet another lie attributed to the Prophet ﷺ is the saying "When the Zanj is hungry, he steals, and when he is full, he fornicates". Ibn Hibban, ibn Adi, ibn al-Jawzi, and al-Dhahabi all declared this narration to be extremely reprehensible.[88]

Another ridiculous fabrication is "the Zanj is a jackass". This insult has been declared a complete fabrication by *hadith* commentators.[89]

Though these *ahadith* are all declared fabrications, they were obviously forged by those who had anti-Zanj sentiments. These anti-Zanj forgeries are perceived as anti-Blackness by contemporary readers. What

they signify is a particular anti-Zanj sentiment which crept into the era of the Abbasids when forgeries of *ahadith* began to proliferate. Anti-Zanj narrations most likely arose in response to the violent uprising against Abbasid rule in Iraq, famously known as Thawrah al-Zanj.[90]

The 'Raisin Head' Hadith

One particular narration which Black orientalists and anti-Muslim critics point to as evidence that Islam as a faith system is inherently anti-Black is the famous 'raisin head' *hadith*. One version of the narration states, "Hear and obey [the commander] even if an Abyssinian that has a head like a raisin commands you."[91] Another version uses the phrase "Abyssinian slave" not just Abyssinian.[92]

Unlike the previous narrations, which *hadith* scholars declared to be fabrications, the "raisin head" narration is considered to be authentic by al-Bukhari, contained in his *Sahih* which is considered to be the most accurate book of prophetic narrations according to Sunnis. It is worth noting that this tradition is not relayed in the authoritative books of prophetic narrations passed down by the Zaydis and Ibadis, the two schools of thought that are considered to be the closest to Sunnis.

The *hadith*, instead of being viewed as anti-Black, is interpreted to mean that obedience to those in authority and in positions of leadership is not contingent on physical appearance or former status of enslavement of the leaders. This meaning is evident from the practice of the Prophet ﷺ when he appointed Zayd bin Harithah ﵁, an Arab who had Black skin, to be his military commander. After the martyrdom of Zayd ﵁, the Prophet ﷺ appointed Zayd's ﵁ son Usamah ﵁, who was also Black in skin color and had an Abyssinian mother, to be commander. Usamah's ﵁ father and mother were both formerly enslaved.

Besides the issue of skin color, the prophetic narration carries the meaning that irrespective of previous pre-Islamic rivalries among Muslims, when facing an external enemy they are to remain united. It was not lost on the Arabs of that time that they had recently been conquered by the Abyssinians. The Abyssinian commander, Abrahah, occupied Yemen and enslaved Arabs and then attempted to conquer

Makkah. The repelling of the Abyssinian conquerors out of the Hijaz is discussed in the Qur'an:

> *Have you [O Prophet] seen how your Lord dealt with the Companions of the Elephant?*
> *And did not He make their scheme into misguidance?*
> *And He sent them birds in flocks.*
> *Striking them with stones of hard clay.*
> *And He made them like eaten straw.* (Q.105:1-5)

Regarding the usage of terminology "head like a raisin", this may appear to be anti-Black when reading within a contemporary Western framework, but is not necessarily the case when looking at how pre-modern Arabs, especially those around the Prophet ﷺ, used similes to compare things with that which was commonly known or used. As an example, al-Zamakhshari mentioned that Arabs used black to refer to dates,[93] and white to refer to milk,[94] both of these being desired consumables.[95] Ibn Hajar al-'Asqalani's commentary on this *hadith* explained that raisins were well-known and frequently eaten fruit among the Arabs, and that the usage of the term was a rhetorical device of painting a likeness to the predominant hair texture of Black people.[96] In other words, the hair texture of Abyssinians was compared to something which Arabs were familiar with and in fact took benefit from. Though the comparison would be seen as culturally offensive or perhaps laughable in the minds of people in the West today, it would be inaccurate to transpose post-modern cultural sensibilities on how such similes were used and understood in Arabia fourteen centuries ago and to conclude that explicit or implicit racism was intended.

Misinterpretations / Erroneous Religious Opinions Issued by Early Scholars About the "Negro"

On Blacks Marrying Whites Changing Allah's Creation

It also crept into the thought of some Muslims that marriages between Blacks and whites are an unnatural phenomenon, to the extent that such unions were considered by some to be inherently bad. Some drew this incorrect conclusion from a misinterpretation of the verse,

> *"And I [meaning Satan] will mislead them, and I will arouse in them [sinful] desires, and I will command them so they will slit the ears of cattle, and I will command them so they will change the creation of Allah." And whoever takes Satan as an ally instead of Allah has certainly sustained a clear loss.* (Q.4:119)

It is attributed to Tawus bin Kaysan – a Persian from the second generation of Muslims – that he stated this verse meant that a Black woman marrying a white man or a white woman marrying a Black man was changing the creation of Allah ﷻ.[97] Others went further and claimed marriages between Blacks and whites that produced children were part of a Satanic plan to change the creation of Allah ﷻ, meaning racial purity. Al-Shinqiti (may Allah have mercy upon him) in his *tafsir* refuted this misunderstanding that interracial marriages are Satanic means of attempting to change the creation of Allah ﷻ by mentioning that the Prophet ﷺ married Usamah bin Zayd رضي الله عنه, who was Black, to Fatimah bint Qays رضي الله عنها, who was lighter in skin color and from Quraysh, and that Bilal رضي الله عنه married the sister of Abd al-Rahman bin Awf. He also pointed out that in the Maliki school, allegiance and affinity for Muslims (which includes marriage) is general for all Muslims irrespective of ethnic or skin color differences, meaning what is supposed to be primary for Muslims is religious affiliation rather than race or class. Surely the Prophet Muhammad ﷺ would not have arranged and conducted marriages between Black and lighter skinned Arabs if these marriages were pleasing to Satan.

Early Scholarly Statements About the Zanj

There is no doubt that anti-Zanj sentiments existed in early Islamic history, and some scholars were influenced by such. Anti-Zanj bigotry morphed into anti-Black statements from some Muslim intellectuals and we even see anti-Black sentiments in racist state policies. For instance in eighteenth century C.E., the Moroccan Sultan, Isma'il bin al-Sharif, who himself had a Black mother, enslaved a group of Black people to serve as his soldiers and servants even though they were free Muslims, a decision which grossly violated sacred law. His Black army, which specifically did not consist of anyone with Arab or Amazighi paternal lineage, was known as the Army of the Slaves of al-Bukhari (*Jaysh Abid al-Bukhari*).[98] This example, however, came many centuries after the first three generations of Muslims, who are respected as the pious predecessors (*salaf al-salih*). There are some respected imams within the first three generations of Muslims who reportedly spoke about the Zanj, and require context and clarification in the same way that the "raisin head" *hadith* needed context.

The first example is contained in a supplication attributed to Imam Ali bin Husayn bin Ali bin Abi Talib (may Allah's blessings be upon them), who is also famously known as Zayn al-Abidin, meaning the Adornment of Worshippers. In one particular supplication known as Du'a al-Thughur, he reportedly supplicated:

> *O Allah! Include in this* [the du'a] *Your enemies in the regions of the lands from India, the Romans, the Turks, the Khazar, Abyssinia, Nubia, the Zanj, the Slavs, the Daylamites and the other nations of polytheism, those whose names and attributes are concealed, but whom You count in Your cognizance and You oversee through Your power.* [99]

Zanj is mentioned with other Black nations such as Abyssinia and Nubia, as well as the quasi-Blacks of India, the supplication also mentions other nations including the lands of the whites, or those considered foreigners in relation to Arabs. The prayer was directed against those who were hostile to Muslims within the regions identified,

who were polytheists or those who associated partners with Allah ﷻ in general. It was not a du'a against all Zanj nor all the people within the other lands mentioned. This was the understanding of his own descendants, as two of them, Yahya bin Umar bin Husayn bin Zayd bin Ali Zayn al-Abidin and Ali bin Zayd bin Husayn bin Isa bin Zayd bin Ali Zayn al-Abidin, both lived with and stood beside the Zanj in Iraq during the period known as Thawrah al-Zanj.[100]

Another example can be found in the words attributed to Imam Zayd bin Ali bin Husayn bin Ali bin Abi Talib.[101] In a discussion about Imam Zayd's role as a teacher of various scholars, it is stated in *Kitab al-Saffah* that one of his students attributed to him the saying, "The Persian man would be over the Zanj man in virtue – even if they were to all enter Islam – in terms of their attribution and skin color, as is known by people."[102] The statement, on its surface, may appear to show that Imam Zayd – whose mother came from the land of darker skinned people of Sindh – took the position that lighter skinned Persians are inherently superior to the dark skinned Zanj.

The key portion of the statement is "as is known by people", meaning as customarily understood to be by the people at that time. A commentator of this particular portion stated that this virtue was based upon that which was commonly assigned by people in that time and place, meaning Iraq approximately thirteen centuries ago. Zanj, in Iraq at that time, became synonymous with a slave class due to the large number of Zanj slaves who were brought to the region. As mentioned before, Zanj was not a term which encompassed all Blacks. The statement that "known by the people" also does not equal Imam Zayd's agreement that Persians had intrinsic merit over the Zanj, but that many of the people in Iraq assigned a socio-political status to Persians over the Zanj.

Reading these words to mean Imam Zayd recognized the inherent merit of Persians over the Zanj would be contrary to his teachings regarding the merits of people being measured based on their remembrance of and obedience to Allah ﷻ. Even if it was to be taken that he meant the superiority of the Persians over the Zanj, Imam Zayd never claimed infallibility for himself nor the other descendants of Imam Husayn ؑ. He stated:

> We are but similar to regular people. We make mistakes and errors, so ask us, but do not accept from us but what conforms with the Book of Allah and the Sunnah of His Prophet.[103]

To accept that one ethnic group is inherently superior to any other clearly goes against the Qur'an:

> *O people! Surely, We created you from a male and female and made you into nations and tribes that you may know one another. Surely the most honorable of you with Allah are those of you who have most regardfulness. Surely Allah is All-Knowing; All-Aware.* (Q.49:13)

Imam Abu al-Fath al-Daylami, who was a Zaydi scholar and a descendant of the Prophet ﷺ, reiterated regarding the *ayah* above that it means "virtue and honor are by [a persons'] actions not due to lineage".[104]

The last example that we will discuss are the words attributed to Imam Ahmad bin Hanbal (may Allah have mercy upon him), who himself was described as tall and intensely dark (*asmar shadid al-sumrah*) as is a common skin color of many in Sudan.[105] It is relayed that he said pertaining to marriage:

> Questioner: What is your view on an Arab lady marrying [a non-Arab] client?
>
> Imam Ahmad: I distinguish between the two of them. The Arab is compatible for the Arab while Quraysh is compatible for Quraysh.
>
> Questioner: And your view if a Zanj marries from the children of Fatimah?
>
> Imam Ahmad: I despise it. This is the speech of *al-Shu'ubiyyah*.[106]

Given that Imam Ahmad was as dark as the Zanj, his objection should not be read as one related to skin color but an issue of class compatibility when it came to marriage. He did not say that he found marriages between Arabs and the Zanj to be impermissible or forbidden according to sacred law. As it relates to socio-political compatibility between a Zanj and a descendant of Fatimah al-Zahra ﵂, this too has nothing to do with skin color as many descendants of Fatimah ﵂ in this era – such as al-Nafs al-Zakiyyah – were as dark as the Zanj.

Imam Ahmad's mention of *al-Shu'ubiyyah*[107] related to anti-Arab sentiments that had arisen during Abbasid rule in Iraq, that was predominately fomented by Persians. His answers to the questions in context were most likely influenced by the atmosphere of *al-Shu'ubiyyah* in Iraq and not a sign of anti-Blackness as it would be understood by many today. To attribute anti-Black racism to his comment would be to read his words outside of their immediate historical context. Surely Imam Ahmad did not give a legal opinion based on the construct of colorism when he himself would be seen today as a Black Arab, though it does not totally absolve him of holding a negative view of the Zanj.

Companions of the Prophet ﷺ who were Black

Bilal bin Rabah

Bilal bin Rabah was born over four decades prior to the *Hijrah* from Makkah.[108] His mother was Hamamah al-Habashiyyah who was one of the early people to accept Islam in Makkah.[109] Bilal also had a sister who accepted Islam named Ghufayrah , meaning the one who seeks forgiveness often.[110] He was described as being very dark, tall and slender in build.[111]

Bilal was one of the first to embrace Islam in Makkah and openly proclaimed that he was Muslim. Outside of those who lived in the house of the Prophet ﷺ, the first to publicly declare their Islam were Abu Bakr, Bilal, Suhayb, Ammar and his parents Sumayyah and Yasir .[112]

Bilal , who was enslaved at the time, was punished by his master for embracing Islam and rejecting the false idols, *al-Lat* and *al-Uzza*. He was regularly taken out in the blazing sun and tortured by Umayyah bin Khalaf who was a pagan aristocrat from Quraysh. Umayyah informed Bilal that he would stop torturing him if he renounced Islam and gave his allegiance to the idols. Bilal's response while being crushed by heavy stones was "*Ahad! Ahad!*" Even under torture Bilal affirmed that there was only one indivisible deity worthy of worship, who does not have a partner. Waraqah bin Nawfal, the uncle of Khadijah bint Khuwaylid , would encourage Bilal to keep the faith while he was being tortured by saying to him, "*Ahad! Ahad!*, by Allah, O Bilal!" Abu Bakr eventually purchased Bilal's freedom from Umayyah which ended the daily torture.[113] In regards to emancipation, Umar bin al-Khattab said, "Our

master is Abu Bakr, and he freed our master [meaning Bilal]."[114] Umar also said regarding this virtuous emancipation, "This master of ours, Bilal, is *hasanah* from the *hasanat* of Abu Bakr."[115]

Bilal was foremost among the earliest Muslims in service to the Prophet ﷺ, who when in need, would ask, "Where is Bilal?" to which Bilal would reply, "I am here and happy to serve you."[116] Hence, the Prophet ﷺ said, "Bilal is the vanguard of the Abyssinian people."[117]

One of the virtues of Bilal is that he was one of the blessed Muslims who struggled for the sake of Allah ﷻ and migrated from Makkah to Madinah. Once in Madinah, he was the first person to ever call the *adhan*.[118] This honor was bestowed upon him by the Prophet ﷺ who said, "The best person is Bilal, and he is the leader of those who call to prayer."[119] Imam Ahmad bin Hanbal stated that Bilal always accompanied the Prophet ﷺ to call the *adhan* for him, while the Prophet ﷺ was traveling or at home, until he passed away.

Regarding the *adhan*, there is a narration which purports that Bilal mispronounced the *adhan* due to him being an Abyssinian. The report relayed that he said "*Ashadu*" instead of "*Ashhadu*". This narration which is found in some books which lack chains of narration – such as *Ruh al-Bayan fi Tafsir al-Qur'an* by Isma'il Haqqi al-Hanafi and *A'yan al-Shi'ah* by al-Sayyid Muhsin al-Amin – has no basis. First, the narration, which is falsely attributed to the Prophet ﷺ, is not found in any of the books of *hadith* nor early books of Islamic history.[120] It does not exist in *Sahih al-Bukhari, Sahih Muslim, Musnad al-Imam Zayd, Musnad al-Rabi' bin Habib, Tarikh al-Tabari*, etc. Albani stated that it is a fabrication.[121] Not a single companion mentioned that Bilal had a problem calling the *adhan* including mispronouncing the "sheen" in "*Ashhadu*". Second, Bilal was born in Makkah not in Abyssinia. He spoke Arabic as his primary language from an early age, which negates the story that he had a problem pronouncing Arabic letters and words clearly. Third, Bilal was known to be among the most eloquent of people from amongst the generation of the companions.[122] In fact, he composed and recited Arabic poetry in clear and beautiful language. Thus, it is highly unlikely that Bilal, who is the master of the prayer-callers, mispronounced the *adhan* for approximately a decade in front of the Prophet ﷺ.

Like several of the companions who migrated without possessing

material wealth, Bilal ﵁ was impoverished upon arriving in Madinah. He was among a humble group known as the People of the Veranda (*Ahl al-Suffah*) who slept in Masjid al-Nabawi.[123] This group of companions were known for their constant worship and remembrance of Allah ﷻ and their excellent character and spiritual states.[124] The Prophet ﷺ kept constant company with these poor companions, such as Bilal, Salman al-Farsi, and Ammar bin Yasir ﵃.

One day, a group of polytheists who thought that they were better than Bilal ﵁ and the other companions of *Ahl al-Suffah*, walked in on the Prophet ﷺ while he was sitting with these poor companions. Allah ﷻ revealed:[125]

> *And do not send away those who call upon their Lord in the morning and evening seeking His countenance.* (Q.6:52)

Abdullah ibn Abbas ﵁ said that the following verse of the Qur'an refers to companions such as Bilal, Khabab, and Ammar ﵃:[126]

> *And those who emigrated for the sake of Allah after they had been oppressed – We will surely settle them in this world in a good place, and the reward for them in the Hereafter will be greater, if they could know.* (Q.16:41)

Thus, Bilal ﵁ was one of the first believers whom the Prophet ﷺ dressed with spiritual investiture.[127]

Bilal ﵁ later served the Prophet ﷺ as the treasurer who would collect and dispense charity on his behalf. The Prophet ﷺ would have Bilal ﵁ give assistance to those who were naked or unclothed and feed those who were hungry. Allah ﷻ says:

> *Believe in Allah and His Messenger and spend out of that in which He has made you successors. For those who have believed among you and spent, there will be a great reward.* (Q.57:7)

It is said that on the day of Eid after delivering the sermon, the Prophet ﷺ took Bilal ﵁ with him to where the women were sitting and then had

Bilal ؓ spread out a cloth for them to place their donations.[128]

As for Bilal ؓ always being by the side of the Prophet ﷺ, he was one of the 313 companions at the Battle of Badr.[129] On that day during the month of Ramadan, Bilal ؓ confronted Umayyah bin Khalaf on the battlefield, the man who regularly tortured him when he was a slave. Umayyah, in his ignorance yelled to Bilal ؓ, "O son of a Black woman!" Bilal ؓ who called Umayyah the "head of disbelief" had the honor of vanquishing his former torturer on that day.[130]

Regarding Bilal's ؓ marital life, it is narrated that he had four wives, though it is unclear if he was married to them all at the same time. The name of one of his wives is unclear. The first of his marriages was to a woman of Bani Bukayr named Hind. The men of Bani Bukayr came to the Prophet ﷺ and asked him if he had someone to marry a sister of theirs. He responded, "Where are you regarding Bilal?" The men turned away as they were not happy. They came back a second time with the same request and received the same response. Then they came back a third time, and this time they agreed for Bilal ؓ to marry her.[131] In one narration of this event, after the men came back on the third occasion, the Prophet ﷺ said, "Where are you regarding a man [Bilal] from the people of paradise?"[132]

His second wife was Halah ؓ, the sister of Abdal Rahman bin Awf, who was one of the richest companions.[133] There is also a report that he had another wife from Bani Zuhrah, the tribe of the mother of the Prophet ﷺ.[134] His fourth wife was Hind al-Khawlaniyyah ؓ. Regarding this marriage, it is relayed that Bilal ؓ and Khalid ؓ (who was the brother in Islam to Bilal ؓ) desired to marry two women from among the Arabs. Bilal ؓ said to them:

> I am Bilal and this is my brother, two slaves from Abyssinia. We were astray and Allah guided us. We were two slaves then Allah freed us. If you allow us to marry, all praises are due to Allah (Alhamdulillah). But if you refuse us, Allah is Greater (Allahu Akbar).[135]

Hind al-Khawlaniyyah ؓ narrated that when Bilal ؓ would retire for the evening, his prayer was, "O Allah! Forgive me for my slips,

accept my good deeds, and pardon me for my aloofness."[136] All of Bilal's ﷺ wives were Arab women.

Despite being a companion of high standing in Madinah, that did not make him immune from being subjected to bigotry. It is narrated that Abu Dharr al-Ghafari ﷺ said to Bilal ﷺ, "O son of a Black lady!"[137] Bilal's ﷺ mother, Hamamah ﷺ, was Abyssinian and formerly enslaved, while Abu Dharr's ﷺ mother was Arab and had never been enslaved. The statement was not simply an issue of anti-Black racism per se, but also about class and societal status. Abu Dharr ﷺ in fact would be seen today as a Black Arab given that he was described as tall with brown skin.[138] Abu Dharr's ﷺ insult to Bilal ﷺ mentioned his mother, which was also the way that his former torturer Umayyah bin Khalaf used to address him. Abu Dharr's ﷺ words, which upset Bilal ﷺ, reached the Prophet ﷺ. When the Prophet ﷺ next saw Abu Dharr ﷺ he said to him, "Do you think it is acceptable to insult his mother, O Abu Dharr?! You are a man that has the Days of Ignorance in you still."[139] Abu Dharr ﷺ then placed his face in the dirt in front of Bilal ﷺ as an act of atonement for the insult.

Bilal ﷺ accompanied the Prophet ﷺ on the conquest of Makkah (*Fath Makkah*) in which the Muslims who had fled the city during the *Hijrah* were able to return victorious. On this very special day, which took place on 20 Ramadan in the year 8 AH, Bilal ﷺ was given two special honors. When the Prophet ﷺ told Uthman bin Talhah ﷺ to open the doors of the Ka'bah for him, the Prophet ﷺ entered into it along with Bilal ﷺ.[140] After removing the false idols and images representing Ibrahim ﷺ and the angels, the Prophet ﷺ told Bilal ﷺ to call the *adhan*. He was the only companion to have ever had such an honor. While Bilal ﷺ called the *adhan*, an Arab reportedly said, "Allah and His Messenger could not find someone other than this black crow." Then Allah ﷻ revealed to the Prophet ﷺ,

> *O people! Surely, We created you from a male and female and made you into nations and tribes that you may know one another. Surely the most honorable of you with Allah are those of you who have most regardfulness. Surely Allah is All-Knowing; All-Aware.* (Q.49:13)

Ibn Abbas said regarding the words *the most regardful of you*, "In this world, it is Bilal."[141]

Prior to the passing of the Prophet ﷺ, he had a vision in which he said, "I entered into paradise then saw the wife of Abu Talhah and also heard footsteps in front of me. I asked, 'What is this, O Jibril?' He replied, 'Bilal.' "[142]

Upon the passing of the Prophet ﷺ, Bilal could not bring himself to call the *adhan* in Madinah. After the burial of the Prophet ﷺ, Abu Bakr asked Bilal to call the *adhan*. Bilal replied to him, "If you freed me for Allah's sake, then let me go, or did you free me for yourself?" Abu Bakr replied, "I did not free you except for Allah's sake."[143] Bilal then left Madinah to participate in campaigns for the conquest of Syria. Bilal ended up being the first Muslim to call the *adhan* at Masjid al-Haram, Masjid al-Nabawi, and Masjid al-Aqsa.

After the passing of the Prophet ﷺ, Bilal only called the *adhan* once in Madinah. One night the Prophet ﷺ appeared to Bilal in a dream. He said to Bilal, "What is this avoidance, O Bilal, that you have not come to visit me?" Bilal awakened from the dream, distressed, and prepared to set off to Madinah. Upon reaching the grave of the Prophet ﷺ, he began to sob until his face was covered in tears. Then Hasan and Husayn, the grandsons of the Prophet ﷺ approached him. It was said that none looked like the Prophet ﷺ from the torso up than Hasan, and none resembled him more from the waist to his feet than Husayn; thus, their combined presence at the resting place of the Prophet ﷺ was as if he was standing directly in front of the Prophet ﷺ.[144] They asked Bilal if they could hear him call the *adhan*. Upon the request of the noble grandsons of the Prophet ﷺ, Bilal agreed. When he proclaimed in his resounding voice "Allahu Akbar, Allahu Akbar", the people of Madinah came alive with energy, reminded of the days when the Prophet ﷺ was among them. When he said, "Ashhadu an la ilaha illallah," the commotion increased. When he said, "Ashhadu anna Muhammadan Rasulullah," the people wondered if the Prophet ﷺ had returned. Then loud crying could be heard, as Bilal's *adhan* reminded the people of what they had lost when the Prophet ﷺ had passed. It

was said that the people of Madinah had not cried that much since the day of the passing of the Prophet ﷺ.[145]

Bilal returned back to Syria and later became ill. While he was on his deathbed, he said, "Tomorrow, I will return to Muhammad and his party." His wife cried out, "What a painful affliction!" He replied to her, "What a joyous occasion!"[146] Bilal passed away and was reportedly buried in Damascus.[147] It is a disputed matter as to whether he had children as well as if he has descendants living today. And Allah knows best.

Some of the meritorious words said about Bilal by the Prophet ﷺ include:

> Take from the Blacks, for surely there are three from among them that are from the leaders of the people of paradise: Luqman the Wise, al-Najashi, and Bilal the Prayer-caller.[148]

> The leaders of the Blacks are four: Luqman the Abyssinian, al-Najashi, Bilal, and Mihja'.[149]

> Rule is in Quraysh, judgment is in the Ansar, and the *adhan* is in Abyssinia [meaning Bilal].[150]

> The best of men is Bilal, and none follows him except a believer. He is the leader of the prayer-callers, and the prayer-callers will have the longest necks of the people on the Day of Resurrection.[151]

> The vanguard is four: I am the forerunner of the Arabs, Bilal is the forerunner of the Abyssinians, Suhayb is the forerunner of the Romans, and Salman is the forerunner of the Persians.[152]

> I entered into paradise, and I saw the wife of Abu Talhah and heard footsteps in front of me. I asked, 'Who is this, O Jibril?' Jibril replied, 'Bilal.'[153]

The Believers from the Family of al-Najashi

It is narrated that the Prophet ﷺ said, "The leaders of the Blacks are four: Luqman the Abyssinian, al-Najashi, Bilal, and Mihja'."[154] Al-Najashi meant king or emperor in the language of the Abyssinians, not one specific man.[155] During the time of the Prophet ﷺ, al-Najashi referred to Ashamah ؓ, who was the pious ruler of Abyssinia in the era in which the Qur'an was first revealed.[156]

When the first Muslims in Makkah suffered persecution at the hands of the polytheists of Quraysh – which took on a greater intensity following the martyrdom of Sumayyah and Yasir, the parents of Ammar, ؓ – the Prophet ﷺ agreed for two groups of his companions to migrate to Abyssinia. He told them,

> Go to the land of Abyssinia, for surely in it is a king who does not oppress anyone. Stay there until Allah gives you relief from your plight.[157]

Once both delegations of Muslims settled in Abyssinia, Quraysh sent a delegation led by 'Amr bin al-As to present gifts to al-Najashi ؓ, with the hope that he would place the Muslims in the custody of the delegation to bring them back to Makkah. After 'Amr made his representations to al-Najashi ؓ, Ja'far bin Abi Talib ؓ, the spokesperson for the Muslims, was asked to read from the Qur'an. Ja'far ؓ read the beginning of Surah Maryam. Upon hearing the recitation about the birth of Isa ؑ, al-Najashi ؓ began to cry. He then said to Amr, "This [Qur'an] and what came to Musa [and Isa] is like the light of one lamp. By Allah, I will never give them to you!"[158]

The Prophet ﷺ later sent a letter to al-Najashi ؓ. One narration mentioned that the words were:

> With Allah's name, the Merciful Benefactor, the Merciful Redeemer. This letter is from Muhammad the Messenger of Allah to al-Najashi, ruler of Abyssinia. Peace be upon whoever follows right guidance and believes in Allah and His Messenger. I

> testify that there is no god except Allah who is one and has no partner, He who did not take for Himself a female companion nor had a son. And I testify that Muhammad is His servant and His Messenger. I invite you to the call of Allah, for surely, I am His Messenger. Surrender [to Islam] and find peace. *O People of the book, come to terms common between us and you, that we will worship only Allah, and not associate anything with Allah, and that none of us take others for lords instead of Allah.* (Q.3:64)[159]

Al-Najashi ﵁ responded in writing:

> With Allah's name, the Merciful Benefactor, the Merciful Redeemer, to Muhammad the Messenger of Allah from al-Najashi, Ashamah bin Abkar. Peace be upon you, Allah's mercy and His blessings, O Prophet of Allah. There is no god except He who guided me to Islam.
>
> And what follows. Certainly, you conveyed a message to me, O Messenger of Allah, in which you mentioned Isa. By the Lord of the heaven and the earth, surely Isa is not more than what you have said. Certainly, we recognize what you sent to us, and we are close to your cousin and his companions. I testify that you are the Messenger of Allah, the Truthful, the Confirmer of truth. Certainly, I pledge my allegiance to you, and to you through your cousin, and I submit myself to the power of Allah, the Lord of the Worlds. If you wish for me to give you anything, I will do so, O Messenger of Allah. Surely, I bear witness that what you say is the truth.[160]

This is the occasion of how the pious al-Najashi ﵁ embraced Islam. His brother, Dhu Mikhmar ﵁, also embraced Islam,[161] as did his son, Abu Niyzar.[162]

Al-Najashi had the honor of marrying Umm Habibah to the Prophet while she was in Abyssinia and he was in Madinah. The marriage gift (*mahr*) given, which she accepted, was 4,000 dirhams.[163]

Al-Najashi died in Abyssinia without ever meeting the Prophet. When word reached the Prophet of the passing of al-Najashi, he commanded his companions, "Pray for your brother who died in other than your land." They asked, "Who is that, O Messenger of Allah?" He replied, "al-Najashi Ashamah."[164] This is the occasion which set the precedent, followed by many Muslims today, known as *Salah al-Gha'ib* – meaning performing the funeral prayer for the deceased in absentia.

Al-Najashi's brother and son, along with other Abyssinians who became Muslim, migrated to Madinah in the final years of the life of the Prophet. Dhu Mikhmar voluntarily became a servant of the Prophet while Abu Niyzar became a voluntary servant of Fatimah al-Zahra. They dedicated their life to the service of the Messenger and his family.

Abu Niyzar then became the caretaker of a garden in Madinah which was owned by the household of Fatimah. The garden, which was named al-Bughaybaghah, was established as an endowment to feed the poor and wayfarers. After Fatimah's passing, it is narrated that her son Imam Husayn incurred some debt and this news made it to Mu'awiyah bin Abi Sufyan. Mu'awiyah attempted to give Abu Niyzar 100,000 dirham to buy it, but Abu Niyzar refused as it was an endowment established for feeding the needy.[165]

Upon the death of Mu'awiyah, his son Yazid became the ruler. When the Umayyads tried to force Imam Husayn to pledge allegiance to Yazid, he and his partisans left Madinah for Makkah in the night. Once in Makkah, they all fled for Iraq, cutting short their Hajj. Imam Husayn and his companions were eventually encircled at Karbala, where he and all of his male companions except for two were martyred. It is recorded the grandson of al-Najashi and son of Abu Niyzar, named Nasr, was one of the martyrs of Karbala.[166] Another Black man named Jawn bin Huway was also one of the martyrs of Karbala.[167]

Mihja' bin Salih ﵁

Mihja' ﵁ was enslaved in Makkah and was emancipated by Umar bin al-Khattab ﵁. He was among the first Muslims to migrate to Madinah for the sake of Allah ﷻ.[168]

Mihja' ﵁ was among the poor companions of the Prophet ﷺ of whom Allah ﷻ spoke of in the Qur'an:[169]

> *And do not send away those who call upon their Lord in the morning and evening seeking His countenance.* (Q.6:52)

Mihja' ﵁ was one of the 313 companions who participated in the Battle of Badr, during the month of Ramadan with the Prophet ﷺ. On that blessed day, Mihja' ﵁ fell as the first martyr. The Prophet ﷺ stated after seeing him martyred, "Mihja' ﵁ is the master of the martyrs, and he is the first [this day] who will be called to the gate of paradise from this *Ummah*."[170] Mihja' ﵁ is the first in the *Ummah* to be given the title the master of the martyrs followed by Hamzah bin Abd al-Muttalib ﵁ who achieved martyrdom at the Battle of Uhud.

Allah ﷻ revealed the following verses relating to Mihja' ﵁ and those who passed away at Badr:

> *Do people think that they will be left alone by saying 'we believe' and they will not be tested?*
>
> *Most certainly We will test them as those who came before them, so that Allah will know those who are truthful and know those who are untruthful.* (Q.29:2-3)

Al-Wahidi relates:

> Said Muqatil: "This verse was revealed about Mihja', the client of Umar bin al-Khattab, who was the first Muslim to be killed at the Battle of Badr. 'Amr ibn al-Hadrami struck him with a bow which killed him. The Prophet, ﷺ, said on that day: 'The master of all

> martyrs is Mihja'. He will be the first one of this community to be called to the gate of heaven'. His wife and parents were distraught because of his death, and so Allah, exalted is He, revealed about them these verses [Q.29:2-3], explaining that they had to suffer trials and hardship for the sake of Allah, exalted is He.[171]

The Prophet ﷺ reportedly said later on, "The leaders of the Blacks are four: Luqman, and Mihja', Bilal, and al-Najashi."[172]

Umm Ayman

Umm Ayman, whose proper name was Barakah, meaning blessing, was the Abyssinian servant of the Prophet's ﷺ father, Abdullah bin Abd al-Muttalib.[173] She was present with Sayyidah Aminah bint Wahb when she gave birth to the Prophet ﷺ. Abbas bin Abd al-Muttalib composed a poem about this auspicious occasion which Umm Ayman witnessed,

> *And then when you were born, a light rose over the earth*
> *until it illuminated the horizon with its radiance.*
>
> *We are in that illumination and light and those paths of*
> *guidance we break through.*[174]

She was also present with Sayyidah Aminah, when she passed away. Abd al-Muttalib at this point assigned Umm Ayman to be the primary caregiver of the Prophet ﷺ saying to her, "O Barakah! Do not be negligent regarding my son."[175] After Abd al-Muttalib passed away, Abu Talib, the uncle of the Prophet ﷺ, then took the Prophet ﷺ into his home. Due to the love and care received from Umm Ayman, the Prophet ﷺ said, "Umm Ayman is the mother after my mother."[176]

Umm Ayman continued to serve the Prophet ﷺ up until he married Khadijah. Upon his marriage, he freed her from her

servitude.[177] Umm Ayman ﷺ married Ubayd al-Khazraji ﷺ and gave birth to her son, Ayman.[178] She was one of the first people in Makkah to accept Islam.[179]

Following the death of Umm Ayman's ﷺ husband, Ubayd al-Kharaji ﷺ, the Prophet ﷺ said to his companions that if any wanted to marry a woman from the people of paradise then to marry Umm Ayman ﷺ. Zayd bin Harithah ﷺ then married Umm Ayman ﷺ. Zayd ﷺ was an Arab who was described by ibn al-Jawzi as a Black Arab who was short.[180] They had a son named Usamah ﷺ, who was beloved to the Prophet ﷺ as if he was his own grandson; he said of Usamah ﷺ that he was "the beloved son of the beloved".[181]

Umm Ayman ﷺ eventually migrated to Madinah along with her son Ayman ﷺ[182] who later achieved martyrdom for the sake of Allah ﷻ. The Prophet ﷺ used to visit Umm Ayman ﷺ every day to check up on her. He said to her, "You are my mother after my mother."[183] She was also present at the occasion when the Prophet ﷺ performed the marriage of his daughter Fatimah al-Zahra ﷺ to Imam Ali bin Abi Talib ﷺ.

After the death of the Prophet ﷺ, Abu Bakr ﷺ and Umar ﷺ used to regularly visit Umm Ayman ﷺ as the Prophet ﷺ did. There are conflicting reports about her death, some reports stating that she died between five to six months after the death of the Prophet ﷺ and others that she passed away under the government of Uthman bin Affan ﷺ, but Allah ﷻ knows best.[184]

Umm Ayman ﷺ narrated the following statement from the Prophet ﷺ:

> Do not intentionally leave prayer, for whoever intentionally abandons prayer, certainly will be disavowed from the protection of Allah and His Messenger.[185]

Fiddah the Nubian

Fiddah the Nubian was a companion of the Prophet who became a servant of Fatimah al-Zahra. Imam Ja'far al-Sadiq stated that the Prophet personally brought Fiddah to the home of Fatimah al-Zahra in Madinah.[186]

Fiddah was known for her piety and memorized the entire Qur'an. Fatimah al-Zahra was her teacher and mentor. It is narrated that the Prophet taught her this supplication while she was living in the home of Fatimah al-Zahra:

> *O One (Wahid), He who there is nothing like Him that causes everyone to die and annihilates everyone. And You are exalted over Your throne; You do not get tired nor do You slumber.*[187]

Fiddah was a witness and participant of the events in the home of Fatimah that were the reason for the revelation of Surah al-Insan. The narration states that Hasan and Husayn were very ill, so the Prophet along with Abu Bakr and Umar came to visit them. Imam Ali and Fatimah al-Zahra swore an oath that if Allah healed Hasan and Husayn, they would fast for three days out of gratitude.

When Allah healed Hasan and Husayn, Imam Ali and Fatimah al-Zahra, along with Hasan, Husayn and Fiddah, started their first day of fasting. Just before the time to break the fast, a poor man from the Muslims came to the door, as Imam Ali had freshly baked barley bread in his hands. The poor man said, "Peace be upon you, O People of the House of Muhammad! Feed me as Allah has fed you from the tables of paradise." Fatimah al-Zahra proceeded to give the poor man all of the barley bread which was the iftar of everyone in the house fasting that day. On the second day they all fasted again, and at the time of breaking the fast another person came to the door and said, "Peace be upon you, O People of the House of Muhammad! I am an orphan from the children of the Muhajirin. My father was martyred on the Day of al-Aqabah. Feed me as Allah feeds you from the tables of

paradise." Fatimah al-Zahra ﷺ then gave him all of their bread for that day. Thus far, water was all that they had consumed for two days at the time of breaking their fast. On the third day of fasting, a prisoner who was a polytheist came to their door and said, "Peace be upon you, O People of the House of Muhammad. You [meaning Muslims] imprisoned us and treated us harshly, and now do not feed us! Give me some food, for surely I am a prisoner of Muhammad." Fatimah al-Zahra ﷺ then gave him all of their barley bread leaving them with nothing but water with which to break their fasts for a third day.

Thereafter Allah ﷻ revealed the following verses to the Prophet ﷺ It is narrated that this is the occasion of the revelation of Surah al-Insan, which includes Ayat 1-13:

> *Has there [not] come upon man a period of time when he was not a thing [even] mentioned?*
>
> *Surely, We created the human from a sperm-drop mixture that We may try him; and We made him hearing and seeing.*
>
> *Surely, We guided him to the path, be he grateful or ungrateful.*
>
> *Surely, We have prepared for the disbelievers chains and shackles and a blaze.*
>
> *Surely, the righteous will drink from a cup [with heavenly drink] whose mixture is of celestial camphor,*
>
> *A spring of which the servants of Allah will drink; they will make it gush forth in force,*
>
> *They [are those who] fulfill [their] vows and fear a Day whose evil will be widespread.*
>
> *And they give food in spite of love for it to the needy, the orphan, and the captive,*

> *[Saying], "We feed you only for the countenance of Allah. We wish not from you reward nor thanks.*
>
> *"Surely, we fear from our Lord a Day austere and distressful."*
>
> *So, Allah will protect them from the evil of that Day and give them radiance and happiness.*
>
> *And will reward them for what they patiently endured [with] a garden [in Paradise] and silk [garments].*
>
> *[They will be] reclining therein on adorned couches. They will not see therein any [burning] sun or [freezing] cold.* (Q.76:1-13)[188]

After the passing of Fatimah al-Zahra, Imam Ali performed the wedding of Fiddah to Abu Tha'labah the Abyssinian, who passed away shortly after. She later married Abu Mulayk Sulayk. Her son by Abu Tha'labah passed away at a young age.[189] She later accompanied the Hashemites who left Madinah for Iraq during the government of Imam Ali, and it was in Kufah that he was martyred by the accursed Kharijite ibn Muljam.

For the last twenty years of her life, Fiddah only responded to people by citing verses from the Qur'an.[190] Fiddah later accompanied Imam Husayn to Iraq and was with the Hashemites during the massacre at Karbala. When Zayn al-Abidin Ali ibn Husayn and the women from the Hashemites were taken as prisoners and made to travel by foot in the hot desert sun from Karbala to Damascus, Fiddah was also taken prisoner. She later died in Damascus and is buried in Bab al-Saghir cemetery in Damascus.[191]

Al-Aswad al-Habashi ﷺ

A man came from Abyssinia and went to the Prophet ﷺ and asked him if he could make an inquiry. The Prophet ﷺ said, "Ask your question." The man, who was al-Aswad al-Habashi ﷺ, asked:

> O Messenger of Allah! You have merit over us regarding appearance, skin complexion and prophecy. If I believe in similar to what you believe in and perform [righteous] deeds similar to your deeds, will I be with you in paradise?

The Prophet ﷺ replied, "Yes. By He who has my soul in His hand, the brilliance of the Black will be seen in paradise from a journey of a thousand years."

The Prophet ﷺ then said:

> Whoever says "La ilaha ill Allah," he [or she] makes a covenant with Allah. And whoever says, "Subhanallah wa bihamdi," He will have written for him [or her] a thousand good deeds or up to 24,000 good deeds.

Al-Aswad ﷺ then asked, "How can one be doomed after this, O Messenger of Allah?"

The Prophet ﷺ replied:

> Surely a man will come on the Day of Resurrection with deeds which if placed upon a mountain they burden it, then the favor or the blessings of Allah will arise eclipsing all his bad deeds. Then he will be informed of all of it except that Allah will lengthen those good deeds by His mercy.[192]

Then Allah ﷻ revealed the first twenty verses of Surah al-Insan.

As it relates to the revelation of these verses in Surah al-Insan, it is not uncommon for scholars of *tafsir* to narrate more than one occasion

of revelation for certain verses. Hence there are narrations that posit these verses as relating to *Ahl al-Bayt* and others that relate them to al-Aswad al-Habashi ؓ, and Allah ﷻ knows best.

Abu Ruwayhah Khalid al-Habashi ؓ

Khalid bin Rabah ؓ, who was the brother of Bilal ؓ the prayer-caller, was known as Abu Ruwayhah. Ibn Hajar stated that Khalid ؓ was the brother of Bilal ؓ in Islam, not his biological brother. Abu Nu'aym al-Asbahani also held the same view.[193] According to these opinions, it would hold that Khalid's ؓ father was a different Rabah and that his mother was not Hamamah ؓ the mother of Bilal ؓ.

It is widely narrated that Khalid ؓ was with Bilal ؓ when they both sought to get married to two women from among the tribe of Khawlan. The engagement proposals of both were accepted. Adam bin Ali stated that he heard Khalid ؓ the brother of Bilal ؓ the prayer-caller say, "People are of three types: One who keeps the peace, one who is kept safe, and one who afflicts harm."[194]

Khalid ؓ also had a blood brother who was also a companion of the Prophet ﷺ, named Tuhayl ؓ.[195]

Khalid bin al-Hiwari al-Habashi ؓ

It was narrated that Ishaq bin al-Harith said:

> I saw Khalid bin al-Hiwari, a man from Abyssinia that was from the companions of the Prophet, come to his people as his death was about to be upon him. He told them, "Make ghusl for me twice: Wash me from my impurities and wash me because of death."[196]

Mihjanah ﵂

Mihjanah ﵂ was a Black woman who had the honor of sweeping up Masjid al-Nabawi.[197] Details are unavailable as to whether she was Abyssinian, Nubian, or a Black Arab. It is only narrated that she was from the People of Madinah.

It is reported that she regularly cleaned the mosque. The Messenger of Allah ﷺ noticed that he had not seen her. He inquired as to her whereabouts and was subsequently told that she had died. He replied, "Why did you not inform me concerning her?" He then left and prayed the funeral prayer over her.[198]

Shuqran al-Habashi ﵁

Shuqran al-Habashi ﵁ was given to the Prophet ﷺ by Abd al-Rahman bin Awf ﵁ to serve him. He was also known as Salih. It is narrated that he was purchased then freed from enslavement after his participation in the Battle of Badr and thus became a client under the protection of the Prophet ﷺ. He was close to the family of the Prophet ﷺ and was reportedly one of the select persons present during the *ghusl* (washing) immediately after the passing of the Prophet ﷺ as well as his burial. Zayn al-Abidin Ali bin Husayn said, "The Prophet ﷺ was lowered into his *qabr* (grave) by Abbas [his paternal uncle], al-Fadl [the son of Abbas] and Shuqran."[199] Ibn Abbas ﵁ stated the same.[200]

Ubadah bin al-Samit ﵁

Ubadah bin al-Samit ﵁ was born in Yathrib, which later became known as Madinah, and was from one of the prominent Arab tribes of the city, al-Khazraj.[201] He was described as tall in stature and very dark in skin color.[202]

Ubadah ﵁ was distinguished as being one of the early Muslims who was present at the first and second pledges in Aqaba at the hand of the Prophet ﷺ, prior to the *Hijrah*. He was one of the first twelve men of

Madinah to embrace Islam.[203] Ibn Kathir and ibn Ishaq quote Ubadah رضي الله عنه stating the following regarding the first pledge of Aqaba:

> I was among those who attended the first (meeting at) Aqaba. We were 12 men. We pledged allegiance to the Messenger of God by the so-called "women's pledge". That was before war was enjoined. It was to the effect that we would not associate any other with God, we would not steal, nor commit fornication, nor kill our children, nor make false accusations, nor disobey him in anything good. "If you keep to this," he told us, "You shall go to paradise. But if you commit any of these, then God will decide your fate; if He wishes He will either punish you or forgive you."[204]

Ibn Ishaq quotes Ubadah رضي الله عنه explaining the oath taken at the second pledge of Aqaba:

> We pledge ourselves to war in complete obedience to the apostle in weal and woe, in ease and hardship and evil circumstances; that we would not wrong anyone; that we would speak the truth at all times; and that in God's service we would fear the censure of none.[205]

Ubadah رضي الله عنه was known for being valiant and learned. He participated in all of the major battles including Badr, Uhud, Khandaq, and Khaybar. He was also one of the scribes who wrote the Qur'an, besides memorizing it.

Following the battle of Badr, the Muslims of Madinah went to war with a local Jewish tribe, Banu Qaynuqa. Many of the Muslim tribes of Madinah had alliances with the Jews of Madinah, including Banu Qaynuqa. Upon hearing of the belligerence of Banu Qaynuqa towards the Prophet ﷺ and the Muslims, Ubadah رضي الله عنه immediately went to the Prophet ﷺ. He stated that as the leader of his tribe he had renounced his tribe's alliance with Banu Qaynuqa. Others, like Abdullah ibn Ubayy refused to renounce their ties to Banu Qaynuqa. Thereafter

Allah ﷻ revealed about Ubadah's ؓ loyalty to Allah ﷻ, His Messenger ﷺ and the Muslims:

> *Your ally is none but Allah and [therefore] His Messenger and those who have believed – those who establish prayer and give zakah, and they bow [in worship]. And whoever is an ally of Allah and His Messenger and those who have believed – indeed, the party of Allah – they will be the victorious.* (Q.5:52-56)[206]

In relation to the spread of Islam in Egypt, Ubadah ؓ was commissioned to lead the delegation which confronted al-Muqawqis, the emperor of Egypt. Al-Muqawqis initially refused to accept Ubadah ؓ as the head of the delegation due to his black skin. He appealed to Ubadah's ؓ companions, asking them how they could accept a black man as their leader. Ubadah's ؓ companions replied that he was the best of them, the most virtuous and knowledgeable amongst them. Ubadah ؓ then spoke up, undeterred by al-Muqawqis's rejection and censure of Black people. Ubadah ؓ impressed upon al-Muqawqis that they were only there to seek the pleasure of Allah ﷻ, and that they would not be enticed by matters of this world. Upon hearing Ubadah's ؓ speech, al-Muqawqis said to his people around him, "Surely this man and his companions were sent by Allah ﷻ to overturn the earth. I presume that their rule will soon dominate the earth."[207]

Ubadah ؓ eventually settled in al-Sham (Syria). He began to speak up against issues which he deemed to be problematic under the governorship of Mu'awiyah bin Abi Sufyan. Mu'awiyah wrote a letter complaining to the caliph Uthman bin Affan ؓ about Ubadah ؓ stating, "Surely Ubadah is the most troublesome in al-Sham to me and its people."[208] Ubadah ؓ was then summoned to appear in front of Uthman ؓ to answer the allegations against him. Ubadah ؓ responded to the accusations against him by quoting the prophetic narration:

> Torrential will be your affairs after me when men recognize what is wrong, but it will not be disliked for themselves what they recognize. So do not obey

whoever disobeys nor sends astray people from your Lord.[209]

Ubadah ﷺ died in Palestine in 34 AH when he was 72 years old. He was buried in the precincts of Masjid al-Aqsa in Jerusalem.[210]

Zubayd al-Sulami

An elder from the Bani Sulaym said that for ten years, Zubayd would complete reading the Qur'an in one day and night. He said that for another twenty years, he completed the reading of the Qur'an in two days and two nights. He said of Zubayd, "By Allah, certainly light came from his face."[211]

The Witness of the Black Wet-Nurse

It was narrated from Uqbah bin al-Harith that he married Umm Yahya bint Abi Ihab. He then said that an enslaved Black lady came to him and said, "I nursed both of you [meaning Uqbah and Umm Yahya]." He then said, "I mentioned this to the Prophet ﷺ who turned his face away." He said, "I then went to the other side, and told him." The Prophet ﷺ retorted, "How can you presume [that it is fine to keep her as your wife] when she [the Black lady] suckled both of you? I prohibit [your marriage] to her [Umm Yahya]."[212]

This event with the Black wet-nurse relates to two principles within sacred law. The first of these is that the witness of a woman, which includes one who is enslaved, is valid as long as she is known to be upright. The second is that the marriage of a man and a woman who have suckled from the same woman is invalid due to the wet-nurse becoming like a mother to those she suckled. In this case, Uqbah and Umm Yahya were like siblings; hence, the swift proclamation of the Prophet ﷺ that they were divorced from that point.

Part Three

The Virtues of *Ahl al-Bayt* & Blackness

THE PEOPLE of the Prophetic Household, known as *Ahl al-Bayt*, hold the highest status of any family within normative Islam. Their virtues are numerous per the Qur'an and the prophetic narrations. In addition, their merits have been discussed and expounded upon in countless books, beginning in the era of the early pious generations of Muslims to contemporary Islamic scholars. A plethora of virtues and merits about them are expounded upon in the Qur'an, the prophetic traditions, sayings of the first three generations of pious Muslims and Islamic scholars who followed them in excellence. There are varying opinions, however, regarding who is included within the term *Ahl al-Bayt*.

The heart of *Ahl al-Bayt*, as explicitly stated by the Prophet ﷺ, are Ali bin Abi Talib, Fatimah bint Muhammad, Hasan bin Ali and Husayn bin Ali ﷺ. In a number of narrations, with slightly different wording yet similar details, the Mother of the Believers Aishah ﷺ stated that the Prophet ﷺ left home one morning and had with him a cloak which was black from Khaybar. The Prophet ﷺ entered the home of Umm Salamah ﷺ, with his grandson Hasan followed by his other grandson Husayn then Fatimah and Ali ﷺ. Wrapping them all under his cloak, he recited, "*Allah desires but to remove from you filth, People of the Household, and to purify you with a thorough purification.*" (Q.33:33) The Prophet ﷺ then prayed, "O Allah! These are my *Ahl al-Bayt*, so remove from them filth and thoroughly purify them."[213] For half a year after this, the Prophet ﷺ went to the door of Fatimah's ﷺ home at the time of Fajr prayer and said, "*Al-salah*, O *Ahl al-Bayt*! Allah desires but to remove from you filth, People of

the Household, and to purify you with a thorough purification."[214]

At the Farewell Sermon on Mount Arafat, the Prophet ﷺ stated, "Surely I am leaving you that which if you hold on to them, you will never go astray after me: the Book of Allah (Qur'an) and the Mantle (*'Itrah*) of the People of my Household."[215] Several scholars of classical Arabic such as Hibatullah al-Shajari al-Hasani understood *'Itrah* to mean a person's close kin from one's children to his children to his children.[216] Thus the *'Itrah* of *Ahl al-Bayt* includes not only Hasan and Husayn ؓ but also their righteous offspring. Thus, imams and scholars such as Sayyid Musa al-Jawn and his most notable descendant Sayyid Abd al-Qadir al-Jiylani, and Sayyidah Nafisah who was the spiritual guide of Imam Shafi'i (may Allah have mercy upon him), are from the *'Itrah*.

Allah ﷻ and His Messenger ﷺ made loving the *Ahl al-Bayt* a condition for having true faith and obtaining high spiritual status. Allah ﷻ stated, *"Say [to the people O Muhammad!]: I ask no reward from you except love for my close kin."* (Q.42:23) The Prophet ﷺ stated, "By He who holds my soul in His possession, a servant does not truly believe until he loves me, and he does not truly believe until he loves my descendants."[217] He also stated, "Love Allah for that which he has nourished you from His favors, love me for the love of Allah, and love my *Ahl al-Bayt* for the love of me."[218]

Conversely, showing enmity towards *Ahl al-Bayt* reflects a lack of faith and is a form of hypocrisy. The Prophet ﷺ stated, "Whoever curses Ali, certainly curses me."[219]

Sayyid Hasan al-Saqqaf said "it is from hypocrisy to hate Sayyidah Fatimah, Hasan, Husayn and *Ahl al-Bayt*" in regards to the authentic *hadith* directed to Ali ؓ, "Whoever loves you is a believer, but whoever hates you is a hypocrite."[220]

The Prophet ﷺ warned, "By he who holds my soul in His possession, none despise us *Ahl al-Bayt* except that Allah will throw him into the hell-fire"[221] and he also warned, "Whoever insults my descendants, certainly insults me, and whoever insults me, insults Allah. The curse of Allah will be upon him to the fill of the heavens and the earth."[222]

Allah ﷻ also mandated that believers venerate and praise the Prophet ﷺ, and included in this praise the mention of *Ahl al-Bayt*. Allah ﷻ commanded, "*Surely Allah and His angels send prayers upon the Prophet. O you who believe, send prayers upon him and salute him repeatedly with peace.*" (Q.33:56) When Sahabah asked how to send prayers upon the Prophet ﷺ, he replied:

> O Allah! Send prayers upon Muhammad and the Family of Muhammad just as you send prayers upon Ibrahim and the Family of Ibrahim. Surely You are Praised, Magnified.
>
> O Allah! Send blessings upon Muhammad and the Family of Muhammad just as you send blessings upon Ibrahim and the Family of Ibrahim. Surely You are Praised, Magnified.[223]

Sayyid Salih al-Ja'fari (may Allah have mercy upon him) composed lines in a poem about praising the *Ahl al-Bayt* by stating:

> They are *Ahl al-Bayt* of the Chosen One in which there is no likeness of them among ordinary people, the family of the most specially gifted station.
>
> The Most Merciful Exalted and Sublime is He who is pleased with them, The Chosen One is pleased with and the people excessively praise them.[224]

Ibn Qayyim al-Jawziyyah stated that every prophetic narration which is ranked as either authentic or good (*hasan*) relating to the command to send prayers upon the Prophet ﷺ includes mentioning his family.[225] Sayyid Muhammad al-Nasir al-Kattani stated that sending *salah* upon the prophetic Household during *tashahhud* has been firmly established through widespread sound (*al-Mutawatirah*) narrations.[226]

Prophetic narrations about the merits of *Ahl al-Bayt* include:

> The similarity of the People of my Household is like the Ark of Nuh, whoever boards will be safe, and whoever does not will sink.[227]
>
> The People of my Household are safety for the people of the earth just like the stars are safety for the people of the heaven.[228]
>
> Every lineage and connection [on the Day of Judgment] will be cut off except my lineage and my connection.[229]
>
> He said to Ali, Fatimah, Hasan and Husayn ﵃, "I am at war with whoever fights you and at peace with whoever is peaceful with you."[230]

The leading lady of *Ahl al-Bayt* is of course Fatimah ﵂, the beloved daughter of the Prophet ﷺ. It is reported that Imam Malik bin Anas (may Allah have mercy upon him) held the opinion that she is the most virtuous person in the *Ummah* after the Prophet ﷺ.[231] He based this from the authentic *hadith* that states, "Fatimah is a piece of me."[232] Sayyid Abd al-Aziz al-Ghumari (may Allah have mercy upon him) said, "There is no legitimate disagreement from the differing of people and their speech with what was relayed from sound textual evidence from the immaculate Messenger ﷺ concerning the merit of Fatimah ﵂ over all of the women of the worlds."[233] Though it is the view of the majority of people of *tasawwuf* that Fatimah al-Zahra ﵂ is the grand spiritual pole of the *Ummah* after the Prophet ﷺ, the two men to be focused on in the rest of this chapter, before discussing other meritorious Hashemites and their *Blackness*, will be the first and the last of the imams of *Ahl al-Bayt,* Ali bin Abi Talib ﵁ and al-Mahdi.

The chief of *Ahl al-Bayt* after the Prophet ﷺ is Imam Ali bin Abi Talib ﵁. Imam Ahmad bin Hanbal stated that nobody from amongst the generation of companions had more sound prophetic statements of virtue narrated about them than Ali ﵁.[234] Imam Ali ﵁ was born in al-Ka'bah, raised in the house of the Prophet ﷺ and was the first male to

accept Islam. According to ibn Abbas, there is not an *ayah* in the Qur'an that says "O you who believe" except that Ali is the head, noble and leader of them.[235] Given that Imam Ali has an ocean of virtues narrated and mentioned about him, and is the most written about Islamic personality after the Prophet ﷺ, this chapter will not elaborate on his expansive biography but instead touch on the issue of his relationship to *Blackness*.

Based on most of the description narrated about Imam Ali, he would be seen as a Black Arab today, who would easily blend into the North Sudanese people. Muhammad bin Jarir al-Tabari, the prolific historian, exegete, *hadith* scholar, and jurist, narrated that when a man asked Imam Muhammad al-Baqir about the physical description of Imam Ali, he stated, "He was a man with very dark skin (*adam shadid al-admah*)."[236] Ibn al-Jawzi and others also described him with the same wording as the narration by al-Tabari, which is the same skin tone description used for Bilal bin Rabah.[237] Al-Arbili, who was a scholar on the biographies of the 12 imams according to the Imami Shi'ah school of thought, relayed that Imam Ali was "dark brown with a handsome face".[238] The lightest description that can be found in the authoritative biographies of *Ahl al-Bayt* is that "his skin was brown".[239]

Regarding the claim that Imam Ali was not dark and that these narrations are fabrications by the Umayyads to insult him is questionable for a number of reasons. As mentioned previously, as it relates to the Arabs' *Blackness,* light skin was an anomaly among Arabs of the generation of the Sahabah. It is unrealistic to hold the view that Imam Ali – or for that matter most of the twelve imams according to Imami Shi'ah thought – resembled the Persianized depictions that appear in pictures in Iran and other locations today. It is also unlikely that the Umayyads used the physical characteristic of dark skin as an insult, given many among them also had dark skin. Describing anyone as being dark in skin color is only an insult if one holds the false belief that darker skin is an inferior creation of Allah ﷻ and is ugly. This was not necessarily the case with pre-modern Arabs, especially since they saw themselves as being Black or being close to *Blackness*, as discussed previously.

Imam al-Mahdi is the awaited last imam of *Ahl al-Bayt*, and it is said he will appear at the end of time. He is the one who will fill the earth with equality and justice. There are differences as to whether al-Mahdi has already been born or not and if he is or will be a descendant of Imam Hasan bin Ali or Imam Husayn bin Ali ﷺ. What is agreed upon by the schools of thought within Sunni and Shi'i theology and the different spiritual paths among Sunnis is based upon the words of the Prophet ﷺ, that "al-Mahdi will be from my offspring, from the children of Fatimah".[240]

Regarding al-Mahdi's appearance, it is narrated that Imam Ali bin Abi Talib ﷺ said, "he is from me from Quraysh, dark or brown [in skin color]."[241] The Hanbali scholar, al-Safarini, stated the same and added that his skin color will be that of the true Arabs.[242] But Allah ﷻ knows best.

The physical appearance of al-Mahdi has consequences due to outward and inward reasons. It is not a benign issue. Those who do not know the signs of al-Mahdi – including his physical appearance – may not accept him when he proclaims himself and asks for their pledge of allegiance, and those plagued by racism or colorism may not accept al-Mahdi due to his skin color being dark. Either or both of these factors could be catastrophic.

Biographies of the *Ahl al-Bayt*

Imam Ali Zayn al-Abidin

Imam Ali Zayn al-Abidin bin Husayn bin Ali bin Abi Talib (may Allah's blessings be upon them) was born in Madinah in 38 AH during the government of his grandfather, the righteous caliph, Imam Ali bin Abi Talib ﷺ.[243] His mother was a Persian lady by the name of Shahzanan.[244] Another opinion is that her name was Ghazalah.[245] He was described as being short in stature with brown skin.[246] He was known as al-Sajjad, meaning the one who was always making prostrations to Allah ﷻ. He was given the title of Zayn al-Abidin, meaning the Adornment of Worshippers. These titles were given to him as it is reported that every day and night he would pray 1,000 *ra'kat*.[247] He did not leave the night vigil (*Qiyam al-Layl*) whether at home or away.[248] This was the view relayed by Imam Malik bin Anas.[249]

Within the schools of *tasawwuf*, Imam Zayn al-Abidin is listed in the chains of transmission of the several spiritual orders. To Zaydis, Zayn al-Abidin is considered an imam of knowledge who possessed high spirituality. Within Ithna'ashari Shi'ah belief, he is the fourth of the twelve immaculate imams. He has two works attributed to him, *al-Sahifah al-Sajjadiyyah*, a collection of supplications for different occasions as well as daily litanies, and *Risalah al-Huquq*, a treatise on different rights that Muslims owe Allah ﷻ and different persons based upon their social relationships. Ibn Sa'ad stated that Imam Zayn al-Abidin was a trustworthy narrator of prophetic traditions and a scholar. Sunni and Shi'i *hadith* collections narrate *hadith* from him.

Imam Zayn al-Abidin was a loved and highly respected leader among the second generation of Muslims. When Abdullah ibn Abbas ﷺ would see him, he would say, "Welcome, the beloved son of the beloved."[250] Al-Zuhri, who transmitted traditions to Imam Malik bin Anas, stated, "I have not seen a Hashemite more virtuous than Ali bin Husayn. I have not seen anyone more comprehending of the religion than him."[251]

Imam Zayn al-Abidin was a witness to the catastrophe of Karbala on 10 Muharram 57 AH, when his father, his father's companions, and his siblings were martyred. Zayn al-Abidin was the only male child of Imam Husayn ﷺ to survive the massacre. He lived with Allah's ﷻ permission due to being unable to fight that day because of severe illness. He, along with his female relatives, was captured and taken in chains from Iraq to Damascus, Syria.

The ruler, Yazid ibn Mu'awiyah, eventually sent Zayn al-Abidin to Madinah, where he was kept under government surveillance. From this point, he devoted his life to teaching sacred knowledge and serving the poorest families in Madinah. None was known to be as generous as him in Madinah. One example of his preference of others over himself is when he visited Muhammad bin Usamah bin Zayd bin Harithah (may Allah be pleased with them) while he was on his deathbed. He saw that Muhammad bin Usamah was weeping profusely. When he inquired as to why, Muhammad bin Usamah said that he had a debt of 15,000 dinars which he feared he could not repay. Such was the piety of Muhammad bin Usamah that he cried because he did not want to die holding so much debt. Zayn al-Abidin took away his sorrows and told him that he would assume the debt and pay it.[252] This is but one example of the generosity of this sayyid from the Prophet's ﷺ household.

Regarding his complete reliance on Allah ﷻ, a group of men found that a fire was burning the home of Zayn al-Abidin. They entered and said, "Fire, Fire, O Son of the Messenger of Allah!" He did not raise his head from prostration until the fire was extinguished. When asked why he did not raise his head, he replied to them that he was more concerned about the fire of the Hereafter.[253]

When Zayn al-Abidin performed the Hajj, he entered into Masjid al-Haram and the people flocked around him. Hisham bin Abd al-Malik,

who was from the ruling class, was also present. The people of Syria asked him who the people were flocking to, and Hisham replied that he did not know the man. The Persian poet Farazdaq, who was also present, told the people of Syria that he knew who the man was. Farazdaq then recited an improvised, 36-line epic poem in praise of Zayn al-Abidin. Some of the lines he recited included:

It is someone whose footsteps are known by every place,
And it is he who is known to the bayt [the Ka'bah] in Mecca,
the most frequented sanctuary;

It is he who is the son of the best of all men of God [The Prophet],
and it is he who is the most pious and devout,
the purest and most unstained,
the chastest and most righteous,
a symbol [for Islam]

This is Ali [bin al-Husayn] whose parent is the Prophet,
this is the son of Fatimah, if you do not know who he is;

Whosoever recognizes his God knows also the primacy and
superiority of this man,
Because the religion has reached the nations through his House.[254]

Hisham bin Abd al-Malik was angered by this praise of Zayn al-Abidin and ordered Farazdaq be arrested while still on Hajj. Zayn al-Abidin sent 12,000 dirhams for the release of Farazdaq from jail.[255]

It was the practice of Zayn al-Abidin to secretly give charity to the 100 poorest households that he knew of in Madinah. He would leave bread on their doorsteps during the night. The People of Madinah were unaware as to the identity of the one leaving the bread until after Zayn al-Abidin passed away, when they stopped receiving their bread.[256]

Zayn al-Abidin was martyred at the age of 57 due to poisoning by the Umayyads.[257] He is buried in al-Baq'i cemetery in Madinah in close proximity to his uncle Imam Hasan bin Ali bin Abi Talib ﵁. Masjid Zayn al-Abidin in Cairo, Egypt, is believed to be the location of the head

of his son, Imam Zayd, though some believe that Zayn al-Abidin's head is also in this location along with his son's.[258]

Zayn al-Abidin reportedly had 16 children.[259] His descendants who reside in Africa today primarily extend from his two grandsons, Imam Musa al-Kazim and Sayyid Ali al-Uraydi (may Allah's blessings be upon both of them).[260]

From his wise sayings:

> Certainly, love is exile.[261]
>
> The worship of the free is being grateful of Allah, not being fearful nor desiring [His reward].[262]
>
> Surely Allah loves the sinful, repentant believer.[263]

Imam Muhammad al-Baqir

Imam Muhammad al-Baqir bin Ali bin Husayn bin Ali bin Abi Talib (may Allah's blessings be upon them) was born in Madinah in 57 AH during the government of Mu'awiyah bin Abi Sufyan. His grandfather Imam Husayn عليه السلام was martyred approximately three years after his birth.[264] His mother was Fatimah bint Hasan bin Ali bin Abi Talib.[265] He was described as being moderate in stature, meaning not very tall nor short, with brown skin.[266] He was also described as being dark or brown in skin color with kinky hair.[267]

Within the schools of *tasawwuf*, Imam al-Baqir is listed in the chains of transmission of several spiritual orders. To Zaydis, Imam al-Baqir is considered an imam of knowledge who possessed deep knowledge of Islamic jurisprudence. Within the Ithna'ashari Shi'ah school, he is the fifth of the twelve immaculate imams.

He is known by the titles of al-Shakir, meaning the one who gives thanks, and al-Hadi, meaning the one who guides. He is most known, however, by the title al-Baqir, meaning the one who splits knowledge open.[268] It is narrated that the name al-Baqir, which was given to him

by the Prophet ﷺ, was a prophetic miracle. It is narrated that the noble companion Jabir bin Abdullah al-Ansari ؓ came to Ali Zayn al-Abidin while his young son al-Baqir was with him. Jabir ؓ said, "O Muhammad [al-Baqir]! Muhammad the Messenger of Allah ﷺ sends you Salam." He then related that the Prophet ﷺ said to him:

> O Jabir! My [grand]son Husayn will give birth to a son, and his name will be Ali. And on the Day of Resurrection a caller will call him saying, 'Rise, O Leader of the Worshippers [*Sayyid al-Abidin*].' And he will have a son, and his name will be Muhammad. O Jabir! When you meet him, give him my Salam.[269]

And the Prophet ﷺ said to Jabir ؓ, "He will be the elucidator of knowledge [al-Baqir], so when you see him, read to him my Salam."[270] This is how Imam al-Baqir got his title.

Imam al-Baqir was known as a scholar and one who was constantly in worship of Allah ﷻ. After the passing of his father, Imam al-Baqir carried on his legacy by teaching sacred knowledge. Ibn Sa'ad mentioned him as being a trustworthy narrator of prophetic traditions.[271] His students who transmitted from him include his brother Imam Zayd, his son Imam Ja'far al-Sadiq, Jabir bin Yazid al-Ju'fi, and Abu al-Jarud. One of his most famous students was Imam Abu Hanifah.[272]

During the reign of the Umayyad tyrant Hisham bin Abd al-Malik, Imam al-Baqir's brother, Imam Zayd, was summoned for interrogation. During the exchange, Hisham started to insult Imam al-Baqir in front of his brother. Hisham said, "What is it that your brother al-Baqarah (the Heifer) does?" Imam Zayd replied,

> Surely it is extreme that you differ from the Messenger of Allah. He named him al-Baqir while you call him al-Baqarah. Surely both of you will differ on the Day of Resurrection. He will enter paradise while you will enter into the hellfire.[273]

Imam al-Baqir had two wives, Umm Farwah who was the granddaughter of Abu Bakr ﵁, and Umm Hakim al-Thaqafiyyah. From these two wives, he had five sons, he also had three additional children from two women who were emancipated from enslavement.[274]

Imam al-Baqir's son, Sayyid Ali, was martyred in Kashan, Persia, during an attack launched by the Umayyad governor of Qazwin. The location of his martyrdom is in the area of Kashan known today as Mashhad Ardahal.[275] Imam al-Baqir's brother Imam Zayd was later martyred on the order of Hisham bin Abd al-Malik in Kufah.[276] Imam al-Baqir was also martyred due to poisoning by the Umayyads.[277] He is buried in al-Baq'i cemetery in Madinah, next to his father Zayn al-Abidin.

From his wise sayings:

> O my son! Beware of laziness and annoyance, for surely both of them are keys to every mischief. Surely when you are lazy, you will not support truth. And when you are annoyed, you will not remain patient upon the truth.[278]

> Something from arrogance does not enter into a heart of a person except that it lessens their intellect similar to what entered, more or less.[279]

> The weapon of an immoral person is profane speech.[280]

> By Allah, the death of a scholar is more beloved to Satan than the death of 70 pious worshippers (who are not scholars).[281]

> A brother to me in my eyes is magnificent, and He who made him magnificent in my eyes made the world (*dunya*) insignificant in his eyes.[282]

> May Allah's mercy be upon the slave that brought alive knowledge. That he remembers with it the

People of Religion and the People of Scruples.[283]

The month of Ramadan is the month of burning away sins. And those who fast in it are guests of Allah and the people of His generosity. Whoever enters into the month of Ramadan fasting in its days, stands in remembrance in its nights and avoids what Allah has made impermissible, he will enter into paradise without reckoning.[284]

To everything is an imperfection, and the imperfection of knowledge is forgetfulness.[285]

The scholar that benefits from his knowledge is better than a thousand [pious] worshippers.[286]

The weightiest of matters are three: The remembrance of Allah in every condition, being equitable even if against yourself, and sharing your wealth with your needy brother.[287]

When you see a Qur'an reciter loving the wealthy, he is a companion of the world (*dunya*), and when you see the ruler holding on to for himself other than what is necessary, he is a thief.[288]

Whoever has been given good character and kindness, certainly he has been given good, all of it, repose and beauty in his spiritual state in his worldly life and his afterlife.[289]

Surely my brother Zayd will revolt [against a tyrant], then will be murdered for being upon the truth. Woe to whoever betrays him, woe to whoever fights him, and woe to whoever kills him.[290]

From some of his explanations of verses of the Qur'an:

> Regarding *"And from men is he who sells himself seeking the pleasure of Allah, and Allah is merciful with His worshippers."* (Q.2:207) he said, "It was revealed pertaining to Ali bin Abi Talib when he humbled himself for Allah and His Messenger on the night in which he laid in the bed of the Messenger of Allah when the disbelievers of Quraysh came to kill him."[291]

> Regarding *"So whoever disbelieves in Taghut and believes in Allah,"* (Q.2:256) he said, "Whoever preoccupies you away from the study of truth, he is your *Taghut* [one who takes away from proper worship]."[292]

> Regarding *"They will wish to exit from the hellfire, but they will not exit from it, and for them is an enduring punishment"* (Q.5:37) he said, "O Jabir! These are the leaders of oppression and their partisans."[293]

Imam Ja'far al-Sadiq

Imam Ja'far al-Sadiq bin Muhammad al-Baqir bin Ali bin Husayn bin Ali bin Abi Talib (may Allah's blessings be upon them) was born on a Monday 17 Rabi' al-Awwal in 83 AH in Madinah.[294] His mother was Umm Farwah Fatimah bint al-Qasim bin Muhammad bin Abi Bakr al-Siddiq (may Allah have mercy upon them).[295] He was given the title al-Sadiq as he was known to be truthful in words and actions.[296] He was described as having light brown skin and black kinky hair.[297]

Imam al-Sadiq is listed in the spiritual chains of transmission of some of the schools of *tasawwuf,* is considered a prominent imam of knowledge in the Zaydi school of thought, and is the sixth immaculate imam according to the Isma'ili and Ithna'ashari Shi'ah. His son, Imam Musa al-Kazim, is considered to have been his spiritual successor. Imam al-Kazim's transmission was passed on to his brother Imam Ali al-Uraydi according to the Ba'Alawi Sufi order, which is predominant

today in Hadramawt, Yemen.[298] A number of books have been attributed to Imam al-Sadiq, though their authenticity has been questioned by scholars. Among these books are *Misbah al-Shari'ah*, the compilation of which has been attributed to al-Fudayl bin Iyad (may Allah have mercy upon him), and *Kitab al-Tawhid* and *Al-Haft al-Sharif min Fada'il Mawlana Ja'far al-Sadiq* both compiled on the authority of Mufaddal bin Umar al-Ju'fi (may Allah have mercy upon him). Mufaddal's compilations of these two books, as well as others, were gathered in the late twentieth century by Ustadh Muhammad al-Khalili and is entitled *Min Amali al-Imam al-Sadiq*. Twentieth century Azhari scholar Shaykh Muhammad Abu Zahra also wrote a book which is a collection of views and statements of the imam entitled *al-Imam al-Sadiq: Hayatuh wa Asruh wa Ara'uh wa Fiqhuh.*

Imam al-Sadiq was praised extensively for his knowledge and his trustworthiness as a transmitter of prophetic narrations, which he narrated from his father and grandfather.[299] Imam Malik bin Anas, Shafi'i, Sufyan al-Thawri, Abu Hatim al-Razi, al-Nasa'i, and ibn Hibban (may Allah have mercy upon them) all considered him to be a highly trustworthy narrator.[300] Al-Dhahabi stated that he was one of the imams of high knowledge and a pious truthful man of great honor, despite al-Bukhari not narrating from him.[301] The students of Imam al-Sadiq include luminaries such as Imam Malik, Imam Abu Hanifah, Sufyan bin 'Uyaynah, Sufyan al-Thawri, Abu Yazid al-Bastami, and Shaqiq al-Balkhi (may Allah have mercy upon them).

As Imam al-Sadiq was born during the era of Umayyad dynastic rule, under the reign of Abd al-Malik bin Marwan, he grew up in an era of oppression of the Hashemites as well as scholars who did not agree with Umayyad governmental decrees and actions. He lived through the rule of Umayyad tyrant Hisham bin Abd al-Malik who was responsible for the martyrdom of his brother Sayyid Ali al-Tahir (may Allah's blessings be upon him) and later his uncle, Imam Zayd (may Allah's blessings be upon him). Imam al-Sadiq said of his uncle's brutal martyrdom:

> May Allah repudiate whoever rejected my uncle. He, by Allah, was the most read of us regarding the Book of Allah, the most knowledgeable of us in the religion

> of Allah, the most dutiful in keeping family ties. By Allah, there is not one left among us in this world and nor in the Hereafter like him.[302]

He also lived through the martyrdom of his cousin, Imam Yahya bin Zayd (may Allah's blessings be upon him), who was also decapitated like Sayyid Ali and Imam Zayd. Imam Yahya's martydom took place during the tyrannical reign of the Umayyad ruler al-Walid bin Yazid bin Abd al-Malik.[303]

After the Umayyad dynasty came the Abbasid dynasty, which surpassed the repression of the Umayyads. After the failed uprising of al-Nafs al-Zakiyyah against the Abbasid sultan Abu Ja'far Abdullah, known by his supporters as al-Mansur, Imam al-Sadiq's life was in danger. It is narrated that the sultan, al-Mansur, sent a man by the name of al-Rabi' (may Allah have mercy upon him) to bring Imam al-Sadiq to him, so that he could have him killed. Al-Rabi', being a lover of *Ahl al-Bayt*, informed Imam al-Sadiq of the threat to his life. Before entering upon the sultan the imam supplicated, "There is no might nor power except with Allah, the Exalted, the Magnificent. I seek assistance by Allah." Imam al-Sadiq ended up surviving that encounter.[304]

Unfortunately, the sultan eventually achieved his goal, and Imam al-Sadiq achieved martyrdom by being poisoned in 148 AH.[305] He was buried in al-Baqi' in Madinah next to his father, grandfather, and Imam Hasan bin Ali ﷺ. His grave was once considered the center of al-Baqi' for Muslims to make visitation throughout the day and night, until the destruction of his shrine by the followers of Muhammad bin Abd al-Wahhab.[306] From his progeny, his great-grandson Hisham bin Husayn bin Ibrahim later migrated to North Africa and then to al-Andalus.[307] Some of his other descendants settled in Fes which is now in modern day Morocco.

The theological and jurisprudential rulings of Imam al-Sadiq as well as his statements of spiritual wisdom are prolific, including:

> Everyone who says that Allah is upon a thing, in a thing, or from a thing is a disbeliever.[308]
> He [Allah] punishes those who do evil, commensurate

to what they have done, and He rewards those who do good with goodness according to it.[309]

In regards to the statement of Allah, *"Regard Him as He should be rightfully regarded,"* (Q.3:102) Imam al-Sadiq said that this means "Regardfulness (*taqwa*), that you do not see in your heart anything equal to Him".[310]

When Imam al-Sadiq was asked about the verse, *"Fair-seeming for them was the evil of their deeds,"* (Q.9:37) he replied that it means ostentation or showing off (*al-riya*).[311]

He said that *Yasin* as mentioned in the Qur'an refers to the Prophet. Imam al-Sadiq stated, "O Sayyid, an address to the Prophet, for surely the Prophet said, "I am your sayyid." He was not praising himself with those words, but he was informing us of the correct meaning of His speech *Yasin*". (Q.36:1)[312]

In it [the Qur'an] is clarification for everything.[313]

The meaning of *"Peace be upon the Family (Il or Aal) of Yasin"* (Q.37:130) is the Family of Muhammad.[314] (This interpretation is based on reciting the Qur'an in Qalun which states "Peace be upon Aal Yasin."[315])

We [*Ahl al-Bayt*] are the Rope of Allah, which Allah the Most High said, *"Hold on tightly together to the Rope of Allah, and do not divide yourselves."* (Q.3:103)[316]

Seek knowledge even to China. Surely knowledge is gnosis of the self, and in it is gnosis of the Lord, Mighty and Sublime.[317]

Surely, we [*Ahl al-Bayt*], by Allah, do not know all that

we are asked while we do not change what is most known to us.[318]

Whoever sends *salah* upon Muhammad and his *Ahl al-Bayt* 100 times, Allah will take care of for him 100 needs.[319]

The scholars are the trustees of the messengers [of Allah]. So, when you see scholars inclined towards governmental authorities, take them to task.[320]

The sword is the key to paradise and the hell-fire.[321]

One who enjoins good and forbids evil should have three [proper] traits: a learned person in what to enjoin and what to forbid, a just person in what to enjoin and what to prohibit, and a tender person in what to enjoin and what to prohibit.[322]

Shaqiq al-Balkhi asked Imam al-Sadiq about chivalry (*al-futuwwah*). He replied, "What do you say about it, O Shaqiq?" He responded, "Chivalry is when given, be grateful and when denied, be patient." Imam al-Sadiq told him, "Dogs also do this. Chivalry is but when given, give away and when denied, be grateful."[323]

Imam al-Sadiq asked Abu Hanifah, "Who is the intellectual?" He replied, "The one who can distinguish better what is good and what is harmful." Imam al-Sadiq replied, "Beasts are also able to distinguish what is harmful to them and what will give them fodder." Abu Hanifah then asked, "Who is the intellectual according to you?" Imam al-Sadiq responded, "The one who distinguishes between two good things and two evils though he chooses from two

good things the better of the two or who has to choose from two evils the better one of the two."[324]

He told Abu Hanifah, "It has been relayed to me that you make analogies [in religious interpretation]. Do not do that for surely the first who made analogical comparison was Satan."[325]

If something reaches you about your brother which you dislike, find for him one to seventy [meaning many] excuses. And if you cannot find an excuse then say surely there must be an excuse for him, but I do not know it.[326]

The best of your youth are those who imitate their elders while the worst of your elders are those who imitate your youth.[327]

There is no provision greater than *al-taqwa*, nothing more beautiful than silence, no enemy more harmful than ignorance, and no malady more infectious than lying.[328]

A believer, when he gets angry, does not let his rage take him away from truth. And when he is happy, he does not let his bliss lead him into falsehood.[329]

The most challenging of adversaries to a believer is a wicked spouse.[330]

Regarding the supplication, *"Our Lord, grant us in this world excellence,"* (Q.2:201) Imam al Sadiq said that this carries the meaning of righteous companionship.[331]

Imam Isa bin Zayd

Imam Isa bin Zayd bin Ali bin Husayn bin Ali bin Abi Talib (may Allah's blessings be upon them) was born in the month of Muharram in 109 AH during the government of Hisham bin Abd al-Malik.[332] His mother was a Nubian lady who was emancipated from enslavement.[333] His birth took place as his father went to confront Hisham bin Abd al-Malik. While traveling on the road, they came across a Christian monastery. His mother went into labor that night; thus, his father named him after al-Masih Isa bin Maryam ﷺ.[334]

Imam Isa was known for his knowledge, scruples, courage and asceticism. He narrated prophetic narrations from his father, his cousins Imam Ja'far al-Sadiq and Sayyid Abdullah bin Muhammad as well as Sufyan al-Thawri, Hasan bin Salih bin Hayy, and Imam Malik bin Anas.[335] He transmitted *hadith* to his son who compiled a collection of prophetic traditions known as *Ra'b al-Sad' Amali al-Imam Ahmad bin Isa bin Zayd bin Ali bin Husayn bin Ali bin Abi Talib* which is one of the most authoritative books of *hadith* within the Zaydi school of thought.

Imam Isa's uncle, Sayyid Ali bin Muhammad, was martyred during the government of Hisham bin Abd al-Malik. His father was later martyred by the army of Hisham while Imam Isa was still young. His father's head, like Imam Husayn's ﷺ, was decapitated and taken from Iraq to Damascus, where it was gifted to the ruler as a trophy. Imam Zayd's corpse was also pinned naked on a cross. Of the signs of sainthood of Imam Zayd was the miracle of a spider weaving a web over his private parts when he was crucified. After being publicly crucified for four years, his blessed corpse, which smelled sweet like musk, was burned and his ashes disposed of.[336]

The end of Umayyad reign led to a new and more treacherous era under the Abbasid dynasty. When Imam Isa's cousin, al-Nafs al-Zakiyyah, stood up to the tyranny of al-Mansur, he accompanied him. After the martyrdom of al-Nafs al-Zakiyyah, Imam Isa went on to support the uprising of his cousin al-Nafs al-Radiyyah Ibrahim bin Abdillah, serving as the standard-bearer when he was martyred.[337]

Imam Isa was later martyred by the Abbasid ruler Abu Abdullah Muhammad, known to his supporters as al-Mahdi, in 169 AH; he is buried in Kufah, Iraq.[338] He had four sons, Ahmad, Zayd, Muhammad, and Husayn.[339]

Al-Nafs al-Zakiyyah

Imam al-Nafs al-Zakiyyah Muhammad bin Abdillah bin Hasan bin Hasan bin Ali bin Abi Talib (may Allah's blessings be upon them) was born in 93 AH during the government of al-Walid bin Abd al-Malik.[340] His mother was Hind bint Abi Ubaydah.[341] He was described as intensely dark in color.[342] He was known as al-Nafs al-Zakiyyah (the pure soul) but was also known as al-Mahdi (the guided one) due to the *hadith*, "Surely al-Mahdi will be from my descendants, his name will be my name, and his father's name will be that of my father's name."[343] Likewise, there is also a *hadith* making reference to the title al-Nafs al-Zakiyyah being "a man from my children, his name is like my name, and his father's name is like my father's name".[344]

Al-Nafs al-Zakiyyah was known to be an erudite scholar. He memorized the Qur'an and taught it. He was a man of deep comprehension of the religious sciences and was also known for being charitable.[345] It is said that *Kitab al-Siyar* – which is a famous book among the jurists of the Hanafi school of thought – contains many rulings that derive from the transmission of al-Nafs al-Zakiyyah.[346]

During the reign of the Abbasid ruler al-Mansur, tyrannical governance returned to the *Ummah*, which the Abbasids claimed to be reforming after the rule of the Umayyads. Al-Nafs al-Zakiyyah's father Abdullah (may Allah's blessings be upon him) was killed in prison by the Abbasids.[347] His uncle Hasan bin Hasan bin Hasan bin Ali bin Abi Talib (may Allah's blessings be upon them) died in the same prison.[348] Likewise, his uncle al-Abbas bin Hasan bin Hasan bin Ali bin Abi Talib (may Allah's blessings be upon them) died in prison.[349] His son Ali (may Allah's

blessings be upon him) also died while imprisoned. The level of persecution against the descendants of Imam Ali bin Abi Talib ﷺ was so prolific during the time of al-Mansur that there was a special prison for them known as "the prison for the Hashemites".

Al-Nafs al-Zakiyyah called the people of Madinah to swear allegiance to him in his quest to stand up against the tyranny of the Abbasids. The elders and the youth among the Hashemites in Madinah swore allegiance to him. Among them were Husayn and Isa, sons of Imam Zayd bin Ali bin Husayn bin Ali bin Abi Talib, as well as Musa and Abdullah, sons of Imam Ja'far al-Sadiq.[350] Imam Malik bin Anas issued a fatwa in support of his uprising against al-Mansur.[351] Imam Malik would later be arrested and flogged by al-Mansur.

Al-Nafs al-Zakiyyah was later killed in Madinah by the Abbasids in 145 AH. His body was buried in al-Baqi', however, he was decapitated and his head was taken as a trophy to al-Mansur in Iraq.[352] Today there are many people who reside in Morocco who trace their lineage from his great-grandson, Sayyid Hasan al-Qadim bin al-Qasim al-Akbar bin Muhammad al-Nafs al-Zakiyyah.[353]

Ishaq al-Mu'taman

Sayyid Ishaq al-Mu'taman bin Ja'far al-Sadiq bin Muhammad al-Baqir bin Ali bin Husayn bin Ali bin Abi Talib (may Allah's blessings be upon them) was born in al-Urayd, which is slightly outside Madinah. His mother was Humaydah, who was from the Amazighi people.[354] His mother was Black and his father was a brown Arab with kinky hair.

He was a man known for his virtuous character, knowledge and being a sound narrator of prophetic traditions. Sufyan bin Uyyanah said, "I narrated from the trustworthy, the felicitous Ishaq bin Ja'far al-Sadiq bin Ali bin Husayn bin Ali bin Abi Talib."[355] Hence he is known as al-Mu'taman meaning the one who is reliable.

Al-Mu'taman married Sayyidah Nafisah bin Hasan bin Zayd bin Hasan bin Ali bin Abi Talib (may Allah's blessings be upon them) in Madinah. They later left for Egypt in 193 AH[356] and had

two children together: al-Qasim and Umm Kulthum.[357] It is also narrated that he had a son named Muhammad by Umm Kulthum bin Ali bin Umar bin Ali bin Husayn bin Ali bin Abi Talib (may Allah's blessings be upon them), and two sons named Hasan and Husayn by a woman emancipated from enslavement.[358]

Sayyidah Aishah bint Ja'far

Sayyidah Aishah bint Ja'far al-Sadiq bin Muhammad al-Baqir bin Ali bin Husayn bin Ali bin Abi Talib (may Allah's blessings be upon them) was born in Madinah during the rule of the Umayyads. Her mother was Humaydah, who was from the Amazighi people.[359] She was also was known by the nickname of Umm Farwah.[360]

Sayyidah Aishah, like other Hashemites of her time, left the Hijaz and sought refuge in Egypt. She was well-known during her lifetime for her worship and piety.[361] It is said that she was extremely generous towards the poor and never turned away anyone who asked for her assistance.

She passed away in the year 145 AH in Cairo and was buried in a location which now has a mosque named after her.[362] It is not recorded that she ever married or had children.

Imam Musa al-Kazim

Imam Musa al-Kazim bin Ja'far al-Sadiq bin Muhammad al-Baqir bin Ali bin Husayn bin Ali bin Abi Talib (may Allah's blessings be upon them) was born in Madinah in 128 AH during the government of Marwan ibn Muhammad ibn Marwan ibn al-Hakam. His mother, Humaydah, was Amazighi.[363] He was described as having black skin.[364] Of his many noble character traits was generosity. He was considered an upright and trustworthy narrator of *hadiths* and his rank was known among the people of the Sunnah to be "from the Imams of the Muslims".[365] Relating to his worship, he would stand most of the night in prayer. He was referred to as al-Kazim due to his immense capacity to control his anger and hold his

temper despite being excessively wronged. His nickname derives from the words of Allah ﷻ when He said, *"Those who spend [in the cause of Allah] during ease and hardship and who restrain anger* [Kazimina] *and who pardon the people – and Allah loves the doers of good."* (Q.3:134)

Within the schools of *tasawwuf*, Imam al-Kazim is listed in the chains of transmission of several spiritual orders. To Zaydis, Imam al-Kazim is considered an imam of knowledge who possessed high spirituality as reflected in his oft-recited supplication known as *Du'a al-Jawshan*.[366] Within the Ithna'ashari Shi'ah school, he is the seventh of the twelve immaculate imams. There is one book in existence which contains 59 sayings of the Prophet ﷺ and Imam Ali bin Abi Talib ؓ, narrated from Imam al-Kazim named *Musnad al-Imam Musa bin Ja'far* that was compiled by Musa bin Ibrahim al-Maruzi who lived in the third century AH.

While residing in Madinah, Imam al-Kazim's cousin Imam Husayn bin Ali bin Hasan bin Hasan bin Hasan bin Ali bin Abi Talib (may Allah's blessings be upon them) called Muslims to pledge allegiance to him in an uprising against the tyranny and injustices of the Abbasid government. After his cousin and supporters were killed at a location close to Makkah known as Fakh – a tragedy which the Hashemites considered the second Karbala – Imam al-Kazim was summoned to Iraq by the Abbasid ruler, Harun al-Rashid in 164 AH. In Baghdad, many seekers of knowledge began to gravitate towards Imam al-Kazim and became his disciples based upon his gnosis and illuminated character.

An event which highlights the spiritual attraction of Imam al-Kazim relates to an interaction between himself and a learned Abyssinian Christian named Abrahah. Imam al-Kazim asked Abrahah, "How is your knowledge regarding your scripture [the Gospel]?" Abrahah replied, "I am a scholar in it and its interpretation." Then Imam al-Kazim started to recite the Gospel to him. Abrahah then said, "The Messiah most certainly recited it like this, and none recite it like this except the guided one. I have studied this for the past fifty years." He then submitted to Islam at the hands of Imam al-Kazim.[367]

Seen as a threat by Harun al-Rashid, Imam al-Kazim was unjustly imprisoned. While in jail, he achieved martyrdom on 25 Rajab in 163 AH after consuming poisoned rations.[368] The government decreed that his corpse be hung from a bridge in Baghdad for the people to see. This was done to send a message to those who aligned themselves closely with the descendants of Imam Ali bin Abi Talib ﵁, that they would suffer the same fate should they decide to oppose the Abbasid government. His remains were eventually buried in central Baghdad, in the neighborhood known today as al-Kazimiyyah.

Following his martyrdom, his son Imam Ali al-Rida (may Allah's blessings be upon him) succeeded him in leading his family. His saintly sister, Sayyidah Aishah, who had the same father and mother as Imam al-Kazim, passed away before him in 145 AH in Cairo, Egypt.[369] Two of his brothers, Muhammad al-Dibaj and Ali al-Uraydi, left Madinah for Makkah during this politically turbulent time.[370] Most of the descendants of Abu Talib who were living fought alongside Muhammad al-Dibaj against Abbasid tyranny.[371] Muhammad al-Dibaj eventually died in Khurasan while Ali al-Uraydi – whose descendants eventually settled in Hadramawt – died not far outside of Madinah.

One of Imam al-Kazim's sons who became infamous for the extreme way in which he resisted Abbasid tyranny was Zayd al-Nar (the fire). Zayd al-Nar's anger over the rule of al-Ma'mun led him to revolt against the government, setting fire to the homes of the Abbasids in Basrah, Iraq. Another of Imam al-Kazim's son, known as Ibrahim al-Murtada, had a Nubian mother named Najiyyah.[372]

Imam al-Kazim has numerous descendants throughout the Arab world and Persia to this day, though the majority of them still reside in Iraq. His descendants also reside in North Africa, stretching back to his great great-grandson Ja'far bin Muhammad bin Hasan bin Ja'far.[373] For centuries, Imam al-Kazim's grave has been a visiting site for Muslims aiming to draw inspiration and gain blessings. Imam Shafi'i, who was a contemporary of Imam al-Kazim, reportedly encouraged people to visit his burial site and said that it was a remedy and means for supplications to be answered.[374]

Words of wisdom attributed to him include:

> Ishaq bin Ja'far said, "I asked my brother Musa bin Ja'far, 'Can Allah rectify you to be a believer if you are a breaker of promises?' He replied, 'A believer cannot be a habitual liar.' Then he said, 'I relate from my father Ja'far al-Sadiq from his father that he heard the Messenger of Allah say, 'A believer can have every characteristic but not lying nor treachery.' "[375]
>
> Paradise has been forbidden for three types of people: the slanderous gossiper, the drunkard, and the one who sees immorality in his family but stays silent and does not despise it.[376]
>
> Everything has evidence, the evidence of one with sound intellect is deep contemplation, and the evidence of deep contemplation is silence.[377]
>
> Whoever speaks truth with his tongue purifies his actions, and whoever makes excellent his intention will have increased sustenance, and whoever makes excellent his conduct with his brethren and family will extend his life.[378]
>
> The best of what draws a slave closer to Allah after gnosis of Him is *salah* (prayer), good conduct with parents, and abandoning envy, self-absorption, and pride.[379]
>
> A person is not a true believer until he is fearful and hopeful, and he is not fearful and hopeful until his actions are for what he fears and hopes for.[380]
>
> The example of the *dunya* is similar to sea water that is drunk due to thirst which then increases thirst more until it kills.[381]

> To everything is charity, and the charity of the body is supererogatory fasting.[382]

> Your assistance to a weak person is better than giving charity.[383]

Sayyid Musa al-Jawn

Sayyid Musa al-Jawn bin Abdillah bin Hasan bin Hasan bin Ali bin Abi Talib (may Allah's blessings be upon them) was born in Madinah in 130 AH. His mother was Hind bint Abi Ubaydah.[384] She named him al-Jawn due to him having black skin.[385]

Sayyid Musa al-Jawn was known to be an eloquent poet and a man of moral courage. Abdullah, the son of Imam Ahmad bin Hanbal, stated that Sayyid Musa was a righteous man. Al-Dhahabi graded him as being a sound narrator of *hadith*.[386]

Like other descendants of Imam Ali bin Abi Talib ﷺ, Sayyid Musa suffered political persecution under Abbasid rule. His father Sayyid Abdullah was imprisoned by al-Mansur.[387] Sayyid Abdullah was considered to be the shaykh of the Hashemites of his time and was subsequently martyred while in prison by being beaten to death.[388] His brother, al-Nafs al-Zakiyyah, was also martyred during the rule of the Abbasids.

Sayyid Musa al-Jawn left Madinah for Makkah after the martyrdom of his elder brother al-Nafs al-Zakiyyah and his brother al-Nafs al-Radiyyah. While making Hajj, he came across the Abbasid ruler al-Mahdi, and asked him for safety. Among the witnesses to this incident were Sayyid Hasan al-Anwar, Imam Musa al-Kazim, and Hasan bin Ubaydillah bin Abbas bin Ali bin Abi Talib.[389]

Sayyid Musa al-Jawn passed away during the reign of Harun al-Rashid. His descendants reside throughout the world to this day. One group settled in Morocco and al-Andalus.[390] From his descendants was Sayyid Idris bin Musa al-Thani bin al-Shaykh al-Salih Abdillah who had an Amazighi mother known as Umm Majid.[391] Another group of them stayed in the Hijaz as well as settled in Oman; these

are known as the tribe of al-Ukhaydir.[392] Others from among his descendants moved to Persia and Iraq. Perhaps the most famous of the descendants of Sayyid Musa al-Jawn is Sayyid Abd al-Qadr al-Jiylani, the esteemed ascetic and Hanbali jurist, whose shrine is in Baghdad, Iraq.

Sahib al-Daylam Yahya

Imam Yahya bin Abdillah bin Hasan bin Hasan bin Ali bin Abi Talib (may Allah's blessings be upon them) was born during the reign of the Umayyads. His mother was Qураybah bint Abdillah al-Mutallibi.[393] It is narrated that Imam Yahya had dark brown skin, a handsome face, and was short in physical stature.[394]

Imam Yahya lived during the turbulent era of the Abbasid dynasty targeting members of the descendants of Imam Ali bin Abi Talib ﷺ as well as the imprisonment and torture of scholars. Like his siblings, he learned sacred knowledge which included transmitting prophetic traditions from his older brother al-Nafs al-Zakiyyah and his cousin Imam Ja'far al-Sadiq. He transmitted this knowledge to his son Muhammad al-Uthaybi, the jurist Hasan bin Salih bin Hayy, and the renowned imam, Muhammad bin Idris al-Shafi'i.[395] After the three uprisings – two led by his brothers and one by his cousin Imam Husayn bin Ali bin Hasan bin Hasan bin Hasan bin Ali bin Abi Talib, which were put down by the Abbasids – Imam Yahya retreated from the Hijaz for refuge and to seek supporters. These retreats included going to Abyssinia and Yemen. Imam Yahya later received the pledge of allegiance from people in Makkah, Madinah, Yemen and Egypt, in defiance of the rule of Harun al-Rashid.

Imam Shafi'i reportedly gave his pledge of allegience to Imam Yahya.[396] He was subsequently arrested and taken in chains to Harun al-Rashid. He professed his love for *Ahl al-Bayt* through poetry, under trying circumstances, by writing:

> *O Household of the Messenger of Allah!*
> *Love for you is obligatory from Allah in the Qur'an that He revealed.*
> *Sufficient for you is the magnificence of your honor, that he who does not send prayers upon you, there is no salah from him.*[397]

Imam Yahya eventually retreated to Daylam which is in Persia. His popularity during his time in Daylam is the reason he acquired the title Sahib al-Daylam. He was later arrested and taken to Iraq where he was imprisoned. He was martyred in prison by being starved to death. His son Muhammad al-Uthaybi was also martyred in prison in similar fashion.

Imam Muhammad al-Idrisi

Imam Muhammad bin Idris al-Azhar bin Idris al-Akbar bin Abdillah bin Hasan bin Hasan bin Ali bin Abi Talib (may Allah's blessings be upon them) was born in Morocco during the early period of the Idrisid dynasty. His mother was named Hurrah, who was from the nobles of an Amazigh tribe. He was described as having brown skin with very kinky hair.[398] He was the eldest of his father's twelve sons.

The Idrisid dynasty was founded by Imam Idris al-Akbar after he fled the Hijaz to North Africa after the tragedy of Fakh, which is considered to be the biggest calamity to befall the descendants of the Prophet ﷺ after the tragedy of Karbala.[399] Unifying the tribes in Morocco, Imam Idris al-Akbar was given the oath of allegiance by the people during the reign of Harun al-Rashid. He was martyred in 177 AH by poisoning at the command of Harun al-Rashid.[400] His son, Imam Idris al-Azhar, succeeded him and established the city of Fes as the capital of the Idrisid dynasty. Today Fes is commonly known as the City of Saints. Imam Idris al-Azhar passed away in Fes in 213 AH.

Imam Muhammad succeeded his father and ruled for approximately eight years before passing away in 221 AH. He is buried next to his father and his brother, Umar, in Jami' al-Shurafa which is in the heart of Fes.[401] He was succeeded by his son Ali Haydarah who was

named after Imam Ali bin Abi Talib ﷺ. The scholars of the famous al-Kattani family in Morocco are descendants of Imam Muhammad.[402] The famous Sufi saint Abd al-Salam bin Mashish (may Allah have mercy upon him) is also from his descendants.[403]

Imam Muhammad al-Dibaj

Imam Muhammad al-Dibaj bin Ja'far al-Sadiq bin Muhammad al-Baqir bin Ali bin Husayn bin Ali bin Abi Talib (may Allah's blessings be upon them) was born in Madinah during the reign of the Abbasids. His mother Humaydah was from Africa. He was known as al-Dibaj (the elegant) due to his handsome face and attractive appearance as well as his nobility.[404]

Imam al-Dibaj was known to have been a scholar, an ascetic, and a man of generosity, using his money and time to assist people.[405] Students of knowledge sat at his feet to learn prophetic narrations, most of those coming through the chain of transmission of his father, Imam Ja'far al-Sadiq. He used to fast every other day outside of the month of Ramadan, which was the fast of the Prophet Dawud ﷺ.[406]

Imam al-Dibaj agreed with the methodology of his father's uncle, Imam Zayd al-Shahid, that tyrants should be opposed – including by force if need be – and that this should be done by calling people to give allegiance to an imam from *Ahl al-Bayt*.[407]

Imam al-Dibaj called for people to swear allegiance to him to revolt against the tyranny of the Abbasids. When he made this call in Makkah, it is said that 300 men wearing wool robes (as the ascetics donned), pledged allegiance to him.[408] Among those from the descendants of Abu Talib who were with him when he left Madinah for Makkah to call for allegiance to himself were Husayn bin Hasan al-Aftas, Muhammad bin Sulayman bin Dawud bin Hasan al-Muthanna, Muhammad bin Hasan al-Saliq, Ali bin Husayn bin Isa bin Zayd, Ali bin Husayn bin Zayd, and Ali bin Ja'far bin Muhammad.[409] The Abbasid leader, al-Ma'mun, sent an army to Makkah to put down the rebellion, but his army was resoundingly defeated. Al-Ma'mun then tried to negotiate a peace treaty by sending communication through Imam al-Dibaj's brother Imam Ali al-Rida.

Imam al-Dibaj and his supporters left the Hijaz for the region of Khurasan in Persia. He was eventually martyred by poisoning at the order of al-Ma'mun.[410] Al-Ma'mun hypocritically prayed over Imam al-Dibaj, helped lower him into the ground, and did not leave the burial site until Imam al-Dibaj was completely buried.[411]

Some of the children of Imam al-Dibaj stayed in Persia while others went to Iraq and Egypt. Many of his descendants living today reside in Morocco.

Imam Ali al-Rida

Imam Ali al-Rida bin Musa al-Kazim bin Ja'far al-Sadiq bin Muhammad al-Baqir bin Ali bin Husayn bin Ali bin Abi Talib (may Allah's blessings be upon them) was born on 11 Dhul Hijjah in 153 AH in Madinah during the reign of the Abbasid ruler, al-Mansur. His mother was from Africa, described as being either Black Nubian or Abyssinian.[412] Imam al-Rida was described as being dark (*al-jawn*) meaning dark brown to black in skin color or moderately black (*aswad mu'tadil*).[413]

Imam al-Rida is listed in the chains of transmission in some of the schools of *tasawwuf*, is an Imam according to the Zaydi school of thought, and is the eighth immaculate imam according to the Ithna'ashari Shi'ah. His brother, Imam Ibrahim al-Murtada is considered to be the spiritual successor to their father in the chains of transmission of the Rifa'i order.[414] There are two books in existence which can be accurately attributed to Imam al-Rida. The first of these is *al-Risalah al-Dhahabiyyah* which is the first book compiled specifically on the subject of prophetic medicine. The second is *Sahifah al-Imam al-Rida* which is a small compilation of prophetic narrations, sayings of Imam Ali bin Abi Talib ﷺ and his grandson Ali bin Husayn; this book, which is considered authentic in the Zaydi school of thought, primarily contains non-controversial statements of wisdom relating to spirituality and character. A third book attributed to him contains his alleged *fiqh* rulings, *al-Fiqh al-Mansub li al-Imam al-Rida*, which contains some dubious content which cannot be authentically attributed to him.

Imam al-Rida is considered to be a sound narrator among Sunni and Shi'i Muslims. Imam al-Rida narrated the following *hadith qudsi*:

> The statement La ilaha ill Allah is My fortress, so whoever says it enters into My fortress, and whoever enters into My fortress is safe from My punishment.[415]

An alternate version states,

> La ilaha ill Allah is My fortress, so whoever enters into My fortress is safe from My punishment.[416]

Abdullah bin Ahmad al-Maqdisi reportedly said that if the chain of this *hadith qudsi* from Ali al-Rida from his father Musa al-Kazim from his father Ja'far al-Sadiq from his father Muhammad al-Baqir from his father Ali from his father Husayn ﵁ from his father Ali ﵁ from the Prophet ﷺ from Jibril ﵇ from Allah ﷻ, was read over an insane person, that it would bring them out of their insanity.[417] An almost verbatim statement is also attributed to Imam Ahmad bin Hanbal.[418]

Perhaps the most famous student of Imam al-Rida is Ma'ruf al-Karkhi (may Allah have mercy upon him). Ma'ruf is known as al-Karkhi because the neighborhood of Baghdad which he resided in was known as Karkh. He came from a Christian background and accepted Islam, then called his parents to accept, which they did.[419] He is known as one of the foremost gnostics within the early Muslim community, coming after the first three generations.

Imam Ali al-Rida left Iraq for Persia, eventually residing in Niysabur. Abu Hamid al-Ghazali related that in Niysabur the imam resided across from a bathhouse. While in the bathhouse, a man came in and assumed that the imam was a servant working there, presumably because of his black skin. The man then disrobed and commanded the imam to stand to fetch him some water for his bath. The imam stood and did as he was commanded despite not being a bathhouse worker.[420] This is but one testament of the immense humility of Imam Ali al-Rida while also being an example of the biased assumptions which existed at the time in Persia relating to Black

people. While in Niysapur, the imam reportedly narrated the *hadith qudsi* previously mentioned.[421]

After the passing of Harun al-Rashid, civil war broke out among the Abbasids. His son Muhammad al-Amin assumed the throne after his father but was later deposed by his brother Abdullah al-Ma'mun. Al-Ma'mun leveraged the support of Persians, who were disenchanted over perceived Arab chauvinism, when deposing his brother. In seeking to quell unrest among the Arabs as well as the popular resistance against the Abbasids led by descendants of Imam Ali bin Abi Talib ﵁, al-Ma'mun nominated Imam Ali al-Rida to be his political successor. Imam al-Rida was summoned to join al-Ma'mun. The backdrop of this proclaimed succession plan was the competing rival governments to the Abbasids, the Umayyads in al-Andalus, and the Idrisids in Morocco who are the descendants of Imam Hasan bin Ali bin Abi Talib ﵁.

Imam Ali al-Rida was summoned from Niysapur by al-Ma'mun to publically announce that the imam would be his successor. Al-Ma'mun gathered the foremost of the people and proclaimed:

> O people! Surely I see among the Abbasids and the Hashemites that there is none more meritorious for the caliphate nor anyone who has more right to it than Ali bin Musa.[422]

Imam Ali al-Rida was eventually martyred by poisoning during this time of political intrigue.[423] The city in Persia where he is buried, which is known as Mashhad, means the location of martyrdom [of Imam Ali al-Rida]. His grave is located in what is now one of the world's largest mosque and is frequented by millions of visitors annually. It is narrated that the great *hadith* scholar ibn Khuzaymah would make visitation to the burial site of Imam Ali al-Rida to make supplications.[424]

Two of his sisters, who also share his Nubian mother, are Sayyidah Hakimah and Sayyidah Fatimah al-Ma'sumah.[425] Sayyidah Hakimah was known to be one of the most virtuous women of her generation and was a transmitter of *hadith*.[426] Sayyidah Fatimah was also known for her piety and was a transmitter of *hadith* including two famous narrations in which the Prophet ﷺ said, "Whoever I am his master then

Ali is his master," and told Imam Ali bin Abi Talib ﵇, "You are in the position to me as Harun was to Musa."[427] The mosque in Qum, Iran, was constructed at the burial place of Sayyidah Fatimah al-Ma'sumah and is a place of visitation for hundreds of thousands of Muslims every year.[428]

Many of his descendants settled in Iraq and later migrated to al-Andalus. They trace their ancestry to him through Musa bin Abdillah bin Husayn bin Ja'far bin Ali al-Hadi bin Muhammad al-Jawad.[429] Some also later settled in Fes.

Some of his wise sayings:

> Al-Fadl bin Sahl asked Imam Ali bin Musa al-Rida in the assembly of al-Ma'mun: 'O Abu Hasan! Are people compelled to act against their will?' He replied, 'Surely Allah is more just than to compel and then punish.'[430]

> From the character of the prophets is cleanliness.[431]

> True worship is not simply a lot of fasting and praying, but true worship is much contemplation regarding the command of Allah.[432]

> Silence is a gate from the gates of wisdom. Surely silence employs love; surely it is evidence upon every goodness.[433]

> The friend of every matter is intellect while the enemy of it is ignorance.[434]

> Showing love to people is half of intellect.[435]

Imam Muhammad al-Jawad

Imam Muhammad al-Jawad bin Ali al-Rida bin Musa al-Kazim bin Ja'far al-Sadiq bin Muhammad al-Baqir bin Ali bin Husayn bin Ali bin Abi Talib (may Allah's blessings be upon them) was born in Madinah on 10 Rajab in 195 AH during the era of the reign of Abbasid ruler Muhammad al-Amin. His mother was a Nubian woman who was freed from enslavement, and who reportedly descended from the same family as Mariyah al-Qibtiyyah, the mother of the Prophet's ﷺ last-born son Ibrahim.[436] His mother's name was commonly known as al-Sabikah.[437] Imam al-Jawad was primarily described as being intensely dark brown (*shadid al-udmah*).[438] He was known as al-Jawad (the generous) because he was always giving in charity to those who asked as well as to those who did not ask for assistance.[439] He was also known as al-Taqi due to his strict regard for the commandants of Allah ﷻ.[440]

Imam al-Jawad is listed in chains of transmission of some schools of *tasawwuf* and is believed to be the ninth immaculate imam according to the Ithna'ashari Shi'ah.

At a young age, Imam al-Jawad witnessed political intrigue and felt the consequences of it. When his father Imam Ali al-Rida (may Allah's blessings be upon him) was summoned by the Abbasid ruler al-Ma'mun to Iraq, Imam al-Jawad was left behind with his mother in Madinah. After his father left Iraq for Tus, he died from poisoning thus making Imam al-Jawad an orphan. Years after the death of Imam Ali Rida, al-Ma'mun insisted that Imam al-Jawad marry his daughter.[i441]

After al-Ma'mun died, he was succeeded by his younger brother Muhammad al-Mu'tasim, who summoned Imam al-Jawad from Madinah to come to Baghdad. Just as Imam al-Jawad had been left behind by his father with his mother in Madinah, Imam al-Jawad left his son Ali behind with his mother as he was compelled to go to Iraq. Like his father, Imam al-Jawad was killed by being poisoned; he was buried in Baghdad in 254 AH, and his burial site has become a popular destination for spiritual visitation.[442]

Some of his wise sayings:

Reliance upon Allah is salvation from every evil and protection from every enemy.[443]

There are four qualities that assist a person in their actions: sound health, richness, knowledge and ability.[444]

Chastity is the adornment of poverty, gratitude is the adornment of richness and patience is the adornment of affliction.[445]

The scholar working for tyranny, the aider of it and the one who is pleased with it are all partners.[446]

The Day of Justice upon an oppressor will be much more severe than a day of injustice upon the oppressed.[447]

Whoever applauds obscenity is an associate of it.[448]

Every noble is one who dignifies his actions.[449]

Imam Ali al-Hadi

Imam Ali al-Hadi bin Muhammad al-Jawad bin Ali al-Rida bin Musa al-Kazim bin Ja'far al-Sadiq bin Muhammad al-Baqir bin Ali bin Husayn bin Ali bin Abi Talib (may Allah's blessings be upon them) was born in a village outside of Madinah in 214 AH. His mother was an Amazighi woman who was emancipated from slavery, named Sumanah.[450] He was described as having brown skin.[451] He was known as al-Nasih, the one who gives sincere advice, al-Mutawakkil, the one who is reliant, al-Fatih, the one who opens what was closed, and al-Hadi, the one who guides people to right, which is the title that he was most popularly known by.[452]

Imam al-Hadi was known as a pious man, and a scholar. He is listed

in the spiritual chains of some of the schools of *tasawwuf* and is considered the tenth immaculate imam according to the Ithna'ashari Shi'ah. The Shafi'i scholar ibn Hajar al-Haytami stated that he was a man who was known for pious worship, a man of comprehension of Islamic jurisprudence, and that he was a spiritual inheritor of his father's sacred knowledge and generosity.[453] He was also considered a trustworthy narrator of prophetic traditions.

The Abbasids forced Imam al-Hadi to move from the Hijaz to Baghdad, and then placed him under house arrest. He subsequently died of poisoning at the hands of the Abbasids.[454] The shrine in which he is buried in along with his son Imam Hasan al-Askari (may Allah's blessings be upon him) is located in Samarra, Iraq.[455] Visitors frequently come to his place of burial seeking blessings and healing from illnesses by making supplications to Allah ﷻ there.[456]

One of his wise sayings is:

> Surely the forbearing oppressor plots that he will be pardoned for his wrongdoing by his forbearance. Surely the foolish truthteller plans while extinguishing the light of his truth by his foolery.[457]

Imam Hasan al-Askari

Imam Hasan al-Askari bin Ali al-Hadi bin Muhammad al-Jawad bin Ali al-Rida bin Musa al-Kazim bin Ja'far al-Sadiq bin Muhammad al-Baqir bin Ali bin Husayn bin Ali bin Abi Talib (may Allah's blessings be upon them) was born in Madinah between 230 AH and 232 AH during the reign of the Abbasid ruler al-Mu'tazz.[458] His mother was a Nubian woman who was emancipated from slavery, named Sawsan.[459] Imam al-Hadi gave her the name Salil because she was a righteous woman who was free from bad character traits and immoral impurity.[460] Imam al-Askari was described as being brown in skin color.[461]

Imam al-Askari was known for his asceticism as well as his religious knowledge pertaining to difficult matters.[462] He was also a narrator of prophetic traditions, connecting to the Prophet ﷺ through an unbroken

chain of narration from his forefathers. One such narration from Sibt bin al-Jawzi reads:

> My grandfather, Abu al-Faraj, in his book named *'Bi Tahrim al-Khamr'* (The Prohibition of Wine) transmitted from a manuscript, which I also heard him say, 'I swear by Allah that I heard Abu Abdullah Husayn bin Ali say, I swear by Allah that I heard Abdullah bin Ata al-Harawi say, I swear by Allah that I heard Abd al-Rahman bin Abi Ubayd al-Bayhaqi say, I swear by Allah that I heard Abu Abdullah Husayn bin Muhammad al-Daynuri say, I swear by Allah that I heard Muhammad bin Ali bin Husayn al-Alawi say, I swear by Allah that I heard Ahmad bin Abdillah al-Subayi' say, I swear by Allah that I heard Hasan bin Ali al-Askari say, I swear by Allah that I heard my father Ali bin Muhammad say, I swear by Allah that I heard my father Muhammad bin Ali bin Musa al-Rida say, I swear by Allah that I heard my father Ali bin Musa say, I swear by Allah that I heard my father Musa bin Ja'far say, I swear by Allah that I heard my father Ja'far bin Muhammad say, I swear by Allah that I heard my father Muhammad bin Ali say, I swear by Allah that I heard my father Ali bin Husayn say, I swear by Allah that I heard my father Husayn bin Ali say, I swear by Allah that I heard my father Ali bin Abi Talib say, I swear by Allah that I heard Muhammad the Messenger of Allah say, I swear by Allah that I heard Jibril say, I swear by Allah that I heard Mika'il say, I swear by Allah that I heard Israf'il say, I swear by Allah upon the Preserved Tablet (*al-Lawh al-Mahfuz*) that I heard Allah say, "The drinker of wine is like an idol worshipper."[463]

He became known by the title of al-Askari because he grew up next to a military encampment in Samarra, Iraq, after his father was brought there by the Abbasids; Askar in Arabic means military. His other titles were al-Khalis (the sincere for Allah ﷻ) and al-Siraj (the light of a lamp).[464]

Imam al-Askari was killed by poisoning in 260 AH and was buried next to his father Imam al-Hadi in Samarra.[465] Masjid al-Askari is a much frequented location of worship and a place where both Sunnis and Shi'is go to seek blessings. Regarding Imam al-Askari having a son named Muhammad who is the prophesied Mahdi (The Guided One) that will return at the end of time, this is a disputed matter among Muslims.

According to the well-known creed of the Ithna'ashari Shi'ah, the Mahdi is the son of Imam al-Askari who was born over 11 centuries ago and has been in occultation, but will reappear at the end of time to spread justice. According to the Ithna'ashari Shi'ah, a pillar of belief is the infallible imamate of the twelve imams ending with Muhammad the son of Imam al-Askari. One's faith is not complete according to their creed without believing in the twelfth Imam. The belief that Imam al-Askari had a son by the name of Muhammad who is the Mahdi is not exclusively an Ithna'ashari Shi'ah belief. Some of the People of *tasawwuf* among Sunnis also hold this belief. Shaykh al-Shablanji al-Azhari (may Allah have mercy upon him) referred to him as al-Qa'im (the One who stands up for the truth), al-Muntazir (the Awaited One), and Sahib al-Zaman (Master of the Age) as well as al-Mahdi.[466] This was also the position articulated by the Naqshabandi shaykh, Mehmet Nazim al-Haqqani (may Allah have mercy upon him) who passed away in 1435 AH – his most senior representative currently is Sayyid Hisham al-Qabbani who resides in Michigan.

The majority view of the *Ummah*, however, is that Imam Hasan al-Askari is not the father of the Mahdi. The coming of Imam al-Mahdi is a widely held belief among all sects of Muslims, except for the Ibadi school of thought. There have existed scholarly criticisms about many of the reports pertaining to some of the particulars of the coming of the Mahdi as being weak, with some even considered to be complete fabrications. It is stated in *Futuh al-Makkiyyah*, the magnum opus of Muhyi al-Din ibn Arabi, that the Mahdi is "from the children of Fatimah having the name

of the Messenger of Allah ﷺ, and his grandfather being Hasan bin Ali".[467] Imam al-Askari is a descendant of Imam Husayn bin Ali, not Imam Hasan bin Ali. This opinion of ibn Arabi, however, is not based on authentic prophetic traditions. The issue of an imam being in occultation has been criticized, and did not start with the Ithna'ashari belief of the twelfth imam being hidden. For instance, a defunct group known as al-Kaysaniyyah held that Muhammad bin al-Hanafiyyah, the son of Imam Ali, went into occultation.[468] Likewise, another group claimed that Imam Ali al-Hadi was the awaited one who is hidden.[469]

We can gain a clearer understanding of whether the Mahdi was Muhammad bin Hasan by examining the position of his own family members who lived during this lifetime. The first is the opinion of Sayyid Ja'far al-Zaki (may Allah's blessings be upon him), the brother of Hasan al-Askari, after the passing of his brother.[470] He was known to have been an upright and pious man. Had he recognized the belief of 12 infallible imams, and his nephew reportedly being the twelfth imam, he would not have declared the imamate for himself, calling people to pledge allegiance to him. Ithna'ashari Shi'ah's dismiss his claim and have labeled him al-Kadhdhab (The Liar).[471] The other Hashemite position is that Imam Hasan al-Askari never had a son to begin with; thus, there simply is no possibility for the Mahdi to be currently in occultation. Imam Hasan bin Ali bin Hasan bin Ali bin Umar al-Ashraf bin Ali bin Husayn bin Ali bin Abi Talib (may Allah's blessings be upon them) was born in the same year as Imam al-Askari, outlived him by 44 years, and stated that Imam al-Askari left behind no sons.[472] And Allah ﷻ knows best.

Some of his wise sayings are:

> Surely in paradise is a gate called the Gate of Goodness (*al-Ma'ruf*) and none enter it except for people of goodness.[473]

> Whoever is pleased by not being seen as the honored one of an assembly, Allah and His angels will not desist sending *salah* upon him [or her] until they stand up [to depart].[474]

> Anger is the key to every harmful action.[475]
>
> The believer is a blessing for another believer and a proof against a disbeliever.[476]
>
> The heart of an idiot is in his mouth while the mouth of a wise person is in his heart.[477]
>
> Whoever advises his brother in secret certainly beautifies him, while whoever admonishes him in public humiliates him.[478]
>
> Surely you are obligated to enjoin good and forbid evil.[479]

Imam al-Nasir li al-Haqq Hasan bin Ali

Imam Hasan bin Ali bin Umar al-Ashraf bin Ali bin Husayn bin Ali bin Abi Talib (may Allah's blessings be upon them) was born in Madinah in 225 AH.[480] His birth took place during the reign of the Abbasid ruler Muhammad al-Mu'tasim. His mother was Persian and was brought to the Hijaz as a slave and then emancipated. He was described as tall in stature with dark brown skin.[481] He was known as al-Nasir li al-Haqq, meaning the one that helps people towards truth.[482]

Imam al-Nasir li al-Haqq was known for being pious and brave. He was also known to be a learned man of the sacred sciences including theology and prophetic traditions. The prolific historian al-Tabari mentioned that the people of his time did not witness anyone similar to his justice, excellence in his comportment, and his establishment of truth.[483] Regarding his scholarship, it is estimated that he wrote approximately 300 treatises and books ranging from the topics of theology, exegesis of the Qur'an, and sacred law. He was also a master of the Arabic language and poetry. The vast majority of his works are not accessible today, many of them were destroyed and lost while others are only found in manuscript forms in select libraries and in the private possession of sayyids.

Among the books that are available today is *Kitab al-Bisat*, which contains answers to contentious theological issues as well as elucidates on the meanings of words according to the eloquence of the Arabic language. *Kitab al-Bisat* also contains a refutation of the theological deviance of al-Mujabbarah, those who hold the position that all actions of human beings are compelled by Allah ﷻ leaving them without any free will nor agency regarding their ability to act. Their ideas grew in prominence during the time of the second generation of Muslims, and remained an issue in need of refutation especially in teaching converts to Islam. An example of this belief among the people is when a man came to Hasan al-Basri (may Allah have mercy upon him) and stated, "O Father of Sa'id! Surely, I divorced my wife three times. Is there a way out for me regarding this [meaning he wanted her back]?" Hasan al-Basri replied, "Woe to you what made you do that?" The man said, "It was Divine decree." Hasan al-Basri retorted, "You have lied upon your Lord!"[484]

Many of his rulings regarding Islamic sacred law were also preserved by his descendant, al-Sharif al-Murtada, in a book called *Masa'il al-Nasiriyyat*. The book relays opinions of Imam al-Nasir li al-Haqq then gives comments on where al-Sharif al-Murtada disagreed, given that the latter left the path of his forefather for Imami Shi'ism.

Imam al-Nasir li al-Haqq left the Hijaz and eventually settled in Tabaristan in Persia. After coming into political conflict, he then left for the area of Persia known as Daylam. The residents of the region had not yet fully embraced Islam. Through the preaching of Imam al-Nasir li al-Haqq, the inhabitants of Daylam, followers of Zoroastrianism, embraced Islam. Imam al-Nasir li al-Haqq became known in Daylam as al-Utrush, meaning the deaf, after losing his hearing while being tortured and imprisoned. His call to the people of Daylam was:[485]

> O people! Be regardful of Allah and be upright servants of justice exactly as Allah has commanded you to be. Enjoin good, forbid evil, and struggle, may Allah have mercy upon you, for Allah's sake as should be rightfully struggled. Restore good relations with your parents, children, and your brothers [in Islam] for Allah's sake.

Imam al-Nasir li al-Haqq passed away in 304 AH.[486] His shrine in Amul, Iran, is a frequent destination for visitors and those on spiritual retreat.

Some of Imam al-Nasir li al-Haqq's legal opinions include:

> Wiping upon the feet up to the ankles is obligation in *wudu*.[487]
>
> *Wudu* before ghusl is obligatory but afterwards is optional.[488]
>
> *Takbir* (saying Allahu Akbar) in the beginning of the *adhan* is 4 times.[489]
>
> *Tahlil* (saying La ilaha ill Allah) at the end of the *adhan* is one time.[490]
>
> It is not permissible to call the *adhan* for Fajr prior to the rise of Fajr.[491]
>
> The best times for the five daily prayers are when they first come in.[492]
>
> If one reads in Farsi in *salah*, it invalidates their prayer.[493]
>
> Sending *salah* upon the Prophet is part of the first *tashahhud*.[494]
>
> *Qunut* prayer should be made in every prayer that has vocal recitation.[495]
>
> Whoever talks during *salah* out of forgetfulness or knowingly invalidates their prayer.[496]

> Whoever leads the people in *salah* without ritual purity, invalidates his *salah* and the *salah* of the believers.[497]

> It is not permissible to have a known, open transgressor in the position of the imam.[498]

> It is not permitted to break one's fast during Ramadan when traveling except out of necessity.[499]

> There is no *i'tikaf* except with fasting.[500]

> It is not permissible to eat wild donkey meat.[501]

Sayyid Ibrahim al-Murtada

Sayyid Ibrahim al-Murtada bin Musa al-Kazim bin Ja'far al-Sadiq bin Muhammad al-Baqir bin Ali bin Husayn bin Ali bin Abi Talib (may Allah's blessings be upon them) was born during the reign of the Abbasid dynasty. His mother Najiyyah was a Nubian who was emancipated from enslavement.[502] He was known as al-Murtada, meaning the one who attained felicity, after his ancestor Imam Ali bin Abi Talib ﵁.

Sayyid al-Murtada was known for his righteousness, worship, scruples, and virtuous character. He was also a narrator of prophetic traditions.

Unlike most descendants of Imam Ali ﵁ during the reign of the Abbasids, Sayyid al-Murtada lived a long life, passing away in 400 AH. He is buried in his home which is connected to Masjid Husayn in Karbala.[503]

His descendants remained in Iraq after his passing. One of his descendants was Sharif al-Rida who is the compiler of the speeches and maxims of Imam Ali bin Abi Talib ﵁ known as Nahj al-Balaghah. It is relayed that he remained on the Zaydi school of thought, the way of his forefather.[504] Sharif al-Rida's older brother, Sharif al-Murtada, is a famous Ithna'ashari Shi'ah scholar.

Conclusion

THIS WORK has by no means covered all of the prominent Blacks, including Arab Blacks, from among the companions of the Prophet ﷺ, much less covering luminary Blacks from among the second generation of Muslims such as Sa'id bin Jubayr and Mujahid bin Jabr. Many of these illuminated personalities were mentioned in the book which I co-authored *Centering Black Narrative: Black Muslim Nobles*. Moreover, an encyclopedia could be written about the Black Hashemites stretching back to the generation of the companions to the contemporary era, which would include the likes of Imam Ahmad al-Rifa'i, Shaykh Salih al-Ja'fari (may allah have mercy upon them) to Shaykh Muhammad Haydara al-Jilani from Gambia (may Allah preserve him).

What this book attempts to do is not only expand on some of the brief biographies of nobles whom I have written about in the past, but also attempts to counter Orientalist inspired polemics of both Eurocentric academics and Afrocentric critics of Islam; that Islam is an inherently anti-Black religion both theologically and from the very origins of its practice, socially and politically. Thus, not only has the myth of Arab-Black mutual exclusivity been addressed through numerous examples, but clarifications have been presented regarding some controversial, and dare I say blasphemous, narratives that exist in Islamic texts, including from some prolific scholars. These were highlighted not to dismiss the reality of anti-Black racism that exists in some Muslim majority countries – such as the recent enslavement of West Africans in Libya – nor to downplay the existence of colorism within Africa and Asia – colorism in fact pre-dates European colonialism. My interest was to present a more accurate history for the

sake of truth, and to defend the theological integrity of Islam, not the early Muslims' political and religious authorities nor sections of today's general Muslim populace that articulate anti-Black views and hold racist and colorist prejudices which negatively impact darker people.

As we look at the history of Islam as well as contemporary race problems, I do caution not to drown in the sea of secular identity politics, meaning becoming overly consumed with race to the point that race politics becomes our primary concern. As the Prophet ﷺ stated, "For every disease, there is a cure," we have to be cautious about the negative effects on our beings that overmedication can have. Just as taking too much of any literal prescription can lead to toxic side effects, we can also take race consciousness to an extreme, making it a religion in and of itself. This leads to the false practice of abrogating our own spiritual tradition, which includes in it the beautiful character traits of being generous, in giving others the benefit of the doubt, to even pardoning and praying for guidance for those who have harmed us. This side effect can be seen when non-Arab Blacks resort to Arab bashing or Persian bashing polemics. That is not what my discourse is calling for.

As it relates to the inter-tribal and inter-racial relationships between Arabs and non-Arabs, such as Umm Ayman's ﵂ marriage to Zayd bin Harithah ﵁, these examples were used to illustrate that the Prophet ﷺ was involved in and did facilitate such marriages. The children of such marriages were able to gain prominence and acceptance within their society. Likewise, the Prophet's ﷺ noble descendants were also involved in such relationships and marriages which produced many of the prominent scholars of our *Ummah*. These illustrations, however, were not a call towards inviting everyone who is Arab to marry a non-Arab nor for every Black to look for a white spouse. This is not a feasible solution to stave off the marriage crisis that plagues Muslims in the West; single women not finding suitable mates. Nor should people be compelled to give up their preferences if their primary attraction for themselves and their children are pious Muslims within their own ethnic groups.

The discussions about race and how Muslims in the West navigate both external pressures and criticisms and internal challenges need to

continue. I pray to Allah ﷻ that this book adds to the list of written resources that helps us in confronting these issues.

May Allah ﷻ forgive me of any shortcomings, and may He forgive you and all believers. Surely, He is the Oft-forgiving, the Merciful Redeemer.

All praise belongs to Allah ﷻ, the Sovereign, the Truth, and the Clarifier. I bear witness that there is no deity except Allah ﷻ, and I bear witness that Muhammad ﷺ is His slave-servant and His Messenger ﷺ, the keeper of his promise, the trustworthy. O Allah ﷻ! Send prayers and peace upon our leader and master Muhammad ﷺ and upon his purified household and rightly guided companions. We seek refuge with Allah ﷻ from arrogance of racism and from the evils of envy.

Endnotes:

[1] An Arabic term used to denigrate people with black or dark skin. Hans Wehr translates *abd* and *abid* as "slave, serf; bondsman, servant". Wehr, Hans. *Dictionary of Modern Written Arabic: Arabic-English. 4th Revised Edition*, ed. J. M. Cowan (Urbana, Illinois: Spoken Language Services Inc. U.S, 1994), p.685.

[2] Al-'Ayashi, Ahmad. *Kashf al-Hijab 'Aman Talaqa ma'a al-Shaykh al-Tijani min al-*Ashab (Beirut: Al-Maktabah al-Sha'biyyah, n.d.), p.105.

[3] Al-Jiylani, Isma'il. *Al-Fuyudat al-Rabbaniyyah fi al-Maathir wa al-Awrad al-Qadiriyyah* (Damascus: Maktabah Dar al-Duqqaq, 2015), p.92.

[4] Al-Nawawi, Abu Zakariya. *Al-Minhaj fi Sharh Sahih Muslim bin al-Hajjaj* (Beirut: Mu'assasah al-Risalah, 2015), hadith 867.

[5] Al-Suyuti, Jalal al-Din. *Sunan al-Nasa'i bi Sharh al-Suyuti wa Hashiyyahas-Sanadi* (Beirut: Dar al-Ma'rifah, 2008), hadith 1578.

[6] Al-Jahiz, Abu Uthman. *Rasa'il al-Jahiz* (Beirut: Dar al-Kutub al-'Ilmiyyah, 2013), v.1, pp.123-162.

[7] Mubarak, Ahmad, and Dawud Walid. *Centering Black Narrative: Ahl al-Bayt, Blackness & Africa* (Rockford: Itrah Press, 2018), p.2.

[8] Al-Quda'i, Abu Abdullah. *Tarikh al-Quda'i* (Beruit: Dar al-Kutub al-'Ilmiyyah, 2004), p.93.

[9] Ali, Abdullah. *The 'Negro' in Arab-Muslim Consciousness* (Milpitas: Claritas Books, 2018), p.17.

[10] Ibn al-Shajari, Hibbatullah. *Ma Ittafaq Lafzuhu wa Ikhtilaf Ma'nah* (Beirut: Dar al-Kutub al-'Ilmiyyah, 1996), p.144.

[11] Ibn al-Jawzi, Abu al-Faraj. *Tanwir al-Ghabash fi Fadl al-Sudan wa al-Habash* (Riyadh: Dar al-Sharif, 2010), p.228; al-Dhahabi, Shams al-Din. *Siyar A'alam al-Nubala* (Beirut: Mu'assasah al-Risalah, 2015), v.4, p.114.

[12] Al-Jahiz, *Rasa'il al-Jahiz*, v.1, p.157.

[13] Ibn Manzur, Muhammad. *Lisan al-'Arab* (Beirut: Dar al-Sadir, 2010), v.4, p.209.

[14] Al-Jahiz, *Rasa'il al-Jahiz*, v.1, p.158.

[15] Al-Zamakhshari, Mahmud. *Al-Fa'iq fi Gharib al-Hadith*, (Beirut: Dar al-'Asriyyah, 2011), v.1, p.444.

[16] Al-Bukhari, Muhammad. *Sahih al-Bukhari* (Riyadh: Dar ibn Hazm, 2015), hadith 5305; al-Nasa'i, Ahmad. *Sunan al-Nasa'i* (Beirut: Dar al-Kutub al-'Ilmiyyah, 2018), hadith 3480.

[17] Al-Jahiz, *Rasa'il al-Jahiz*, v.1, p.151.

[18] Al-Mu'ayyid, Ali. *Tathqif al-Ummah bi Sirah Awlad al-A'immah* (Beirut: Dar al-'Ilm, 2005), p.282.

[19] Ibid, p.290.

[20] Al-Mu'ayyidi, Majd al-Din. *Al-Tuhf Sharh al-Zalaf* (Sana'a: Mu'assasah Ahl al-Bayt, 1993), p.52.

[21] Al-Asbahani, Abu al-Faraj. *Maqatil al-Talibin* (Beirut: Mu'assasah al-A'alami, 2007), p.428.

[22] Al-Zamakhshari, *al-Fa'iq fi Gharib al-Hadith*, v.1, p.200.

[23] Ibn al-Jawzi, *Tanwir al-Ghabash*, p.236.

[24] Ibn 'Inabah, Ahmad. *Umdah al-Talib fi Ansab Aal Abi Talib* (Beirut: Mu'assasah al-'Ala, 2015), p.74.

[25] Ibn al-Sabbagh, Ali. *Al-Fusul al-Muhimmah fi Ma'rifah Ahwal al-A'immah* (Beirut: Mu'assasah al-A'alami, 1988), p.262.

[26] Al-Qummi, Abbas. *Muntaha al-Amal fi Tawarikh al-Nabi wa al-Aal* (Beirut: Dar al-Mustafa al-'Alamiyyah, 2011), v.2, p.419.

[27] Al-Zu'bi, Abd al-Majid. *Ithaf al-Akabir fi Sirah wa Manaqib al-Imam Muhyi al-Din Abd al-Qadir al-Jiylani al-Hasani al-Husayni wa Ba'd Mashahir Dhurriyatih Uli al-Fadl wa Maathir* (Beirut: Dar al-Kutub al-'Ilmiyyah, 2007), p.134.

[28] Ibn Qudamah, Muwwafaq al-Din. *Al-Mughni* (Riyadh: Dar al-'Alam al-Kutub, 1997), v.9, p.389.

[29] Al-Nawawi, *al-Minhaj fi Sharh Sahih Muslim bin al-Hajjaj*, hadith 520.

[30] Ibn Manzur, *Lisan al-'Arab*, v.4, p209.

[31] Al-Jahiz, *Rasa'il al-Jahiz*, v.1, p.153.

[32] Ibn al-Shajari, Hibbatullah. *Amali bin al-Shajari* (Cairo: Dar al-Khanaji, 2014), v.2, p.325.

[33] Abbad, Isma'il. *Al-Muhit fi al-Lughah* (Qom: 'Alam al-Kutub, 1972), v.3, p.97.

[34] Al-Hakim, Muhammad. *Al-Mustadrak 'ala al-Sahihayn* (Beirut: Dar al-Kutub al-'Ilmiyyah, 2011), hadith 8264.

[35] Al-Jahiz, *Rasa'il al-Jahiz*, v.1, p.155.

[36] Ibn Manzur, *Lisan al-'Arab*, v.2, p.190.

[37] Ibid.

[38] Ibid.

[39] Al-Musawi, Ali. *Amali al-Murtada Ghurar al-Fawa'id wa Durar al-Qala'id* (Beirut: Maktabah al-'Asriyyah, 2009), v.1, p.113.

[40] Al-Zayn, Samih 'Atif. *Tafsir Mufradat Alfaz al-Qur'an al-Karim* (Beirut: Dar al-Kutub al-'Alami, 1994), p.70.

[41] Al-Razi, Muhammad. *Mukhtar al-Sihah* (Beirut: Maktabah Libnan, 1989), p.134.

[42] Ibn Hanbal, Ahmad. *Musnad al-Imam Ahmad bin Hanbal* (Beirut: Mu'assasah al-Risalah, 2001), hadith 3365.

[43] Muslim, ibn al-Hajjaj Abu al-Husayn. *Sahih Muslim* (Riyadh: Bayt al-Afkar al-Dawlah, 1998), hadith 243.

[44] The Night Journey (*Isra* and *Mi'raj*) is a two-part journey during which the Prophet Muhammad ﷺ first travelled on the back of a winged mule-like animal, called Buraq, to al-Aqsa Mosque in Jerusalem, this part of the journey is referred to as the *Isra*. The second part of the journey, the *Mi'raj*, saw the Prophet ﷺ ascend into the seven heavens.

[45] Muslim, *Sahih Muslim*, hadith 239.

[46] The Prophet ﷺ said, "The best of the women of paradise are Khadijah bint Khuwaylid, Fatimah bint Muhammad, Maryam the daughter of 'Imran, and Asiya the daughter of Mazahim, the wife of Pharaoh." Muslim, *Sahih Muslim*, hadith 2185. Allah says in the Qur'an about Asiya ﵂, "*Allah has made an example for those who believe: the wife of Pharaoh when she said, 'My Lord, build a house in the Garden for me in Your presence and rescue me from Pharaoh and his deeds and rescue me from this wrongdoing people.'*" (Q.66:11)

[47] Al-Tabarani, Sulayman. *Al-Mu'jam al-Kabir* (Mosul: Matba'ah al-Zahra al-Hadithah, 1984), hadith 11482.

[48] al-Dhahabi, *Siyar A'alam al-Nubala*, v.1, p.355.

[49] Al-Suyuti, Jalal al-Din. *Kitab Raf' Sha'n al-Hubshan* (Beirut: Dar al-Kutub al-'Ilmiyyah, 2004), p.53.

[50] Al-Tabari, Abu Ja'far. *Tafsir al-Tabari* (Beirut: Dar al-Kutub al-'Ilmiyyah, 1992), v.21, p.68.

[51] Al-Bayhaqi, Abu Bakr. *Shu'b al-Iman* (Beirut: Dar al-Kutub al-'Ilmiyyah, 2008), hadith 1161.

[52] Al-Nu'man, Muhammad. *Al-Ikhtisas* (Najaf: Maktabah al-Saduq, 2009), p.246.

[53] Ibn al-Jawzi, *Tanwir al-Ghabash*, pp.83-4.

[54] Ibid, p.85.

[55] Ibid.

[56] Ibid.

[57] Al-Bukhari, *Sahih al-Bukhari*, hadith 3441; Muslim, *Sahih Muslim*, hadith 171.

[58] Ibn al-Jawzi, *Tanwir al-Ghabash*, p.131.

[59] See for example Surah Yusuf, chapter 12 of the Qur'an. The chapter contains

111 verses and discusses the prophet Yusuf's childhood, his kidnap, life in Egypt, imprisonment all the way to reuniting with his father. The chapter also recounts how the wife of his master (*Aziz*) tried to seduce him. The Qur'an never refers to her by name, yet many exegetes, including al-Razi, al-Tabrisi and al-Zamakhshari, identify her as Zulaykha based on information gained from *Isra'iliyyat* narrations.

[60] Al-Dhahabi, Shams al-Din. *Al-Isra'iliyyat fi al-Tafsir wa al-Hadith* (Cairo: Maktabah Wahbah, 1990), p.14.

[61] Al-Sijistani, Abu Dawud. *Sunan Abi Dawud* (Damascus: Al-Risalah al-'Alamiyyah, 2008), hadith 3284.

[62] Al-Mizzi, Yusuf. *Tahdhib al-Kamal fi Asma al-Rijal* (Beirut: Mu'assasah al-Risalah, 2008), v.17, p.234.

[63] Al-Saqqaf, Hasan, *Sahih Sharh al-Aqidah al-Tahawiyyah* (Cairo: Dar al-Imam al-Nawawi, 1995), p.356.

[64] Al-Bayhaqi, Abu Bakr. *Al-Asma wa al-Siffat* (Cairo: Maktabah al-Taw'iyyah al-Islamiyyah, 2009), p.300; ibn al-Jawzi, Abu al-Faraj. *Majalis ibn al-Jawzi fi al-Mutashabihah min al-Ayat al-Qur'aniyyah* (Beirut: Darl al-Kutub al-'Ilmiyyah, 2013), p.45.

[65] Ibn Khuzaymah, Abu Bakr. *Kitab al-Tawhid wa Ithbat Siffat al-Rabb 'Azza wa Jall* (Riyadh: Dar al-Rushd, 2008), p.122.

[66] *The William Davidson Talmud*, Sanhedrin 108b. https://www.sefaria.org/texts/Talmud [Accessed on 17 June 2020].

[67] Ibn Babawayh, Abu Ja'far. *Ilal al-Shara'i* (Beirut: Mu'assasah al-A'alami, 2007), v.1, pp.38-9.

[68] Al-Ya'qubi, Ahmad. *Tarikh al-Ya'qubi* (Beirut: Mu'assasah al-A'alami, 1993), v.1, p.40.

[69] Al-Quda'i, *Tarikh al-Quda'i*, p.20.

[70] Al-Tabari, Abu Ja'far. *Tarikh al-Tabari* (Amman: Bayt al-Afkar, 2009), p.66.

[71] Al-Zu'bi, *Ithaf al-Akabir fi Sirah wa Manaqib al-Imam Muhyi al-Din Abd al-Qadir al-Jiylani*, p.65.

[72] Ibid, p.67.

[73] Ibn al-Jawzi, *Tanwir al-Ghabash*, p.35.

[74] *[Nuh] said: "O my people! There is no error in me, but I am a Messenger from the Lord of the worlds.* (Q.7:61)

[75] Ibn Hanbal, *Musnad*, hadith 23489.

[76] Al-Tabari, *Tafsir al-Tabari*, v.11, p.398.

[77] Al-Jiylani, Abd al-Qadir. *Al-Ghunyah li Talibi Tariq al-Haqq wa al-Din* (Beirut: Dar al-Khayr, 2005), p.250.

[78] Al-Suhrawardi, Umar. *Awarif al-Ma'arif* (Beirut: Dar al-Kutub al-'Ilmiyyah, 2016), p.196.

[79] Al-Tabari, Abu Ja'far. *Tahdhib al-Athar: Musnad Ali bin Abi Talib* (Cairo: Al-

Mu'assasah al-Sa'udiyyah, 1982), p.104.

[80] Al-Tijani, Ahmad. *Al-Fayd al-Rabbani fi al-Tafsir wa al-Hadith* (Beirut: Dar al-Hadith al-Kattaniyyah, 2012), pp.71-2.

[81] Ibn Hibban, Abu Hatim. *Al-Mujrihin min al-Muhaddithin* (Riyadh: Dar al-Sumayi', 2009), v.1, p.512.

[82] Al-'Asqalani, ibn Hajar. *Lisan al-Mizan* (Beruit: Dar al-Basha'ir al-Islamiyyah, 2002), v.4, p.432.

[83] Al-Kulayni, Muhammad. *Usul al-Kafi* (Tehran: Dar al-Kutub al-Islamiyyah, 1962), v.5, p.352.

[84] Ibn Hibban, *al-Mujrihin min al-Muhaddithin*, v.2, p.298.

[85] Ibn Abd al-Barr, Yusuf. *Al-Tamhid Lamma fi al-Muwatta' min al-Ma'ani wa al-Masanid* (Beirut: Dar al-Kutub al-'Ilmiyyah, 2010, v.19, p.164.

[86] Ibn al-Jawzi, Abu al-Faraj. *Kitab al-Mawdu'at* (Madinah: Maktabah al-Salafiyyah, 1966), v.2, p.628.

[87] Ibn Ali, Zayd. *Musnad al-Imam Zayd* (Beirut: Darl al-Kutub al-'Ilmiyyah, 1999), p.275.

[88] Ibn Hibban, *al-Mujrihin min al-Muhaddithin*, v.2, p.178; ibn 'Adi, Abu Ahmad. *Al-Kamil fi Du'afa al-Rijal* (Riyadh: Maktabah al-Rushd, 2013), v.6., p. 467; ibn al-Jawzi, *Kitab al-Mawdu'at*, v.2, p.627; al-Dhahabi, Shams al-Din. *Tartib al-Mawdu'at* (Beirut: Dar al-Kutub al-'Ilmiyyah, 2009), p.178.

[89] Ibn 'Adi, *al-Kamil fi Du'afa al-Rijal*, v.6., p. 466; ibn al-Jawzi, *Kitab al-Mawdu'at*, v.2, p.233; al-Dhahabi, *Tartib al-Mawdu'at*, p.192.

[90] The Thawrah al-Zanj or Zanj Rebellion was a Black-slave revolt against the Abbasid caliphate. The leader of the rebellion was Ali bin Muhammad, who claimed to be a descendant of Prophet Muhammad ﷺ. Ali bin Muhammad was born in Samarra, Iraq, where he saw the machinations of the Abbasid regime as well as slavery of fellow Muslims throughout Iraq. He eventually left Iraq and moved to Bahrain where he rallied the people to revolt against the Abbasid caliphate. After a failed rebellion attempt being led from Bahrain, Ali bin Muhammad relocated to Basrah, Iraq, in 247 AH where he called the poor people to follow him. His eloquence combined with his lineage attracted followers among the poor in Basrah, which was also a city that had many disenfranchised Blacks who suffered economically and had difficulty getting married. With the support of poor Africans and marginalized Arabs, Ali bin Muhammad unseated the Abbasid authority in Basrah. The Zanj movement had autonomy from the Abbasid caliphate for approximately 15 years before it regained control through brutal force.

[91] Al-Bukhari, *Sahih al-Bukhari*, hadith 693.

[92] Ibid, hadith 7142.

[93] Aishah ﵂ said to Urwa, "O, the son of my sister! We used to see three crescents in two months, and no fire used to be made in the houses of Allah's Messenger ﷺ (i.e. nothing used to be cooked)." Urwa said, "What used to sustain you?" Aishah said, "The two black things i.e. dates and water, except

that Allah's Messenger ﷺ had neighbours from the Ansar who had some milch she-camels, and they used to give the Prophet some milk from their house, and he used to make us drink it." Al-Bukhari, *Sahih al-Bukhari*, hadith 2567. Abdullah bin al-Zubayr bin al-Awwam narrated from his father: "When the following was revealed: *Then on that Day, you shall be asked about the delights!* (Q.102:8) al-Zubair said: 'O Messenger of Allah! Which are the delights that we will be asked about, when they (delights) are but the two black things: dates and water?' He said: 'But it is what shall come.'" Al-Tirmidhi, Abu 'Isa. *Sunan al-Tirmidhi* (Beirut: Dar al-Kutub al-'Ilmiyyah, 2017), hadith 3356.

[94] Abdullah bin Umar narrated the Messenger of Allah ﷺ said, "Al-Kawthar is a river in Paradise, whose banks are of gold, and it flows over pearls and corundum (gems). Its dirt is purer than musk, and its water is sweeter than honey and whiter than milk." Al-Tirmidhi, *Sunan al-Tirmidhi*, hadith 3359.

[95] Al-Zamakhshari, *al-Fa'iq fi Gharib al-Hadith*, v.2, p.202.

[96] Al-'Asqalani, ibn Hajar. *Fath al-Bari Sharh Sahih al-Bukhari* (Cairo: Dar al-Salafiyyah, 2015), v.13, p.107.

[97] Al-Shinqiti, Muhammad al-Amin. *Adwa al-Bayan fi Idah al-Qur'an bi al-Qur'an* (Cairo: Al-Dar al-'Alamiyyah, 2014), v.1, p.493.

[98] Al-Salawi, Ahmad. *Al-Istiqsa li al-Akhbar Duwal al-Maghrib al-Aqsa* (Beirut: Dar al-Kutub al-'Ilmiyyah, 2018), v.1, pp.40-1.

[99] Ibn Husayn, Ali Zayn al-Abidin. *Al-Sahifah al-Sajjadiyyah al-Kamilah* (Baghdad: Maktab Dar al-Kutub al-'Iraqiyyah, 2012), p.82.

[100] Al-Ali, Salih. *Sahib al-Zanj wa Dawlatih al-Mahzuzah* (Beirut: Dar al-Madar al-Islami, 2006), p.46.

[101] Regarding the knowledge of Imam Zayd, his brother, Imam Muhammad al-Baqir, said, "Most certainly Zayd has been given knowledge, and we ask him, for surely he knows what we do not know." (Al-Sayaghi, Husayn. *Al-Rawd al-Nadir Sharh Majmu'a al-Fiqh al-Kabir* (Beirut: Dar al-Jiyl, 2005), v.1, p.112.) Abu Hanifah stated about him, "I have not seen in his time anyone more comprehensive in understanding, nor one more knowledgeable, nor accurately swift in answering, nor more eloquent in speech." (Al-Shablanji, Mu'min. *Nur al-Absar fi Manaqib Aal Bayt al-Nabi al-Mukhtar* (Beirut: Dar al-Kutub al-'Ilmiyyah, 2008), p.300.)

[102] 'Izzan, Muhammad. *Majmu' Kutub wa Rasa'il al-Imam Zayd bin Ali* (Sana'a: Dar al-Hikmah al-Yamaniyyah, 2001), p.183.

[103] Ibid, p.303.

[104] Al-Daylami, Abu al-Fath. *Kitab al-Burhan fi Tafsir al-Qur'an* (Qom: Mu'assasah al-Ba'thah, 2000), p.737.

[105] Ibn al-Jawzi, Abu al-Faraj. *Manaqib al-Imam Ahmad* (Cairo: Dar Hijr, 2008), p.199.

[106] Ibn Hani, Ishaq. *Masa'il al-Imam Ahmad bin Hanbal Rawayah li Ishaq bin Ibrahim bin Hani al-Niysaburi* (Cairo: Dar al-Mawaddah, 2008), p.207.

[107] Hans Wehr translates *Shu'ubiyyah* as "a movement within the early Islamic commonwealth of nations which refused to recognise the privileged position of Arabs". Wehr, *Dictionary of Modern Written Arabic*, p.552. While the term was used to denote nationalism / ethno-centricity, it was originally used as a pejorative against those non-Arab Muslims (pre-dominantly Persians) who refused to recognise the superiority of Arabs. Those identified as *Shu'ubiyyah* referred to themselves as *haraka al-taswiya* (movement of social equality [with Arabs]) Ali, *The 'Negro' in Arab-Muslim Consciousness*, p.125. It is worth noting that the Arabs were not necessarily claiming superiority based on genetic race, but due to cultural factors like the fact that in Islam leadership belonged to the Quraysh (an Arab tribe), the Qur'an was revealed in Arabic, the Prophet ﷺ spoke Arabic, and a Muslim could not fully appreciate his religion without Arabic.

[108] Al-Suyuti, *Kitab Raf' Sha'n al-Hubshan*, p.68.

[109] Al-'Asqalani, ibn Hajar. *Al-Isabah fi Tamyiz al-Sahabah* (Beirut: Maktabah al-'Asriyyah, 2012), pp.1848-9.

[110] Ibid, p.1931.

[111] Ibn al-Jawzi, *Tanwir al-Ghabash*, p.123.

[112] Ibid, p.124.

[113] Al-Suyuti, *Kitab Raf' Sha'n al-Hubshan*, pp.69-71.

[114] Al-Bukhari, *Sahih al*-Bukhari, hadith 3544; ibn al-Jawzi, *Tanwir al-Ghabash*, p.126.

[115] Al-Kurdi, Yusuf. *Al-Intisar li al-Awliya al-Akhyar* (Beirut: Dar al-Kutub al-'Ilmiyyah, 2007), p.330.

[116] Al-Baladhuri, Ahmad. *Ansab al-Ashraf* (Beirut: Dar al-Fikr, 1996), v.1, p.188.

[117] Ibn Sa'ad, Abu Abdullah. *Al-Tabaqat al-Kubra* (Cairo: Maktabah al-Khanaji, 2001), v.3, p.175.

[118] Al-Suyuti, *Kitab Raf' Sha'n al-Hubshan*, p.72.

[119] Al-Asbahani, Abu Nu'aym. *Tahdhib Hilyah al-Awliya wa Tabaqat al-Asfiya* (Beirut: Al-Maktabah al-Islami, 1998), v.1, p.130.

[120] Al-Khadari, Abu al-Khayr. *Juz fi 'Adam Sihhah ma Nuqil 'an Bilal bin Rabah min Ibdalih al-Shin fi al-Adhan Sinan* (Beirut: Dar al-Basha'ir, 2002), p.6.

[121] Albani, Muhammad. *Silsilah al-Ahadith al-Da'ifah wa al-Mawdu'ah* (Cairo: Dar al-Ma'arif, 2008), v14, p.525.

[122] Ibn Kathir, Isma'il. *Al-Bidayah wa al-Nihayah* (Beirut: Maktabah al-Ma'arif, 2016), v.8, pp.304-5.

[123] Al-Hakim, *al-Mustadrak 'ala al-Sahihayn*, hadith 1673.

[124] Al-Asbahani, *Tahdhib Hilyah al-Awliya*, v.1, p.237.

[125] Ibn Kathir, Isma'il. *Mukhtasar Tafsir ibn Kathir* (Beirut: Dar al-Qur'an al-Karim, 1973), v.2, p.134.

[126] Qawuq, Nabil. *Hadha Huwa Bilal – Qira'ah fi Sirah al-Sahabi al-Jalil wa*

'Alaqatih bi al-Nabi wa Ahl Baytih (Beirut: Dar al-Mawaddah, 2016), p.32.

[127] Al-Thamari, Ihsan, and Muhammad al-Qadhat. *Rasa'il min al-Turath al-Sufi fi Labs al-Khirqah* (Amman: Dar al-Razi, 2002), p.121. Spiritual investiture in Sufism (normally with the *khirqah* (the cloak) of the master) is the means by which the disciple becomes part of the silsilah, the chain of mystical succession and transmission, which leads back to the Prophet ﷺ. Most Sufi orders trace their link back to the Prophet ﷺ, through these spiritual investitures back to Ali ﷺ, with some also linking back to Abu Bakr ﷺ. Some mystical leaders claim to have received their *khirqah* directly from al-Khiḍr.

[128] Al-Bukhari, *Sahih al-Bukhari*, hadith 958.

[129] Ibn al-Jawzi, Abu al-Faraj. *Sifat al-Safwah* (Beirut: Dar al-Kitab al-'Arabi, 2008), p.157.

[130] Al-Tabari, *Tarikh al-Tabari*, p.356.

[131] Al-Sijistani, Abu Dawud. *Al-Marasil ma'a al-Asanid* (Beirut: Dar al-Qalam, 1986), hadith 308; al-Bayhaqi, Abu Bakr. *Al-Sunan al-Kubra* (Beirut: Dar al-Kutub al-'Ilmiyyah, 2008), v.7, 137.

[132] Ibn Sa'ad, *al-Tabaqat al-Kubra*, v.3, p.237.

[133] Al-San'ani, Muhammad. *Subul al-Salam Sharh Bulugh al-Maram min Adillah al-Ahkam* (Riyadh: Maktabah al-Ma'arif, 2006), v.3, p.205.

[134] Al-Dhahabi, *Siyar A'alam al-Nubala*, v.1, p.358.

[135] Ibid.

[136] Al-Asbahani, Abu Nu'aym. *Ma'rifah al-Sahabah* (Riyadh: Dar al-Watan, 1998), p.3462.

[137] Al-Majlisi, Muhammad. *Bihar al-Anwar al-Jami'ah li Dirar Akhbar al-A'immah al-Athar* (Beirut: Dar Ihya al-Turath al-'Arabi, 1983), v.22, p.411.

[138] Ibn Sa'ad, *al-Tabaqat al-Kubra*, v.4, p.432.

[139] Al-Bukhari, *Sahih al-Bukhari*, hadith 2545; Muslim, *Sahih Muslim*, hadith 1661; ibn Hanbal, *Musnad*, hadith 21432.

[140] Ibn Hisham, Abu Muhammad. *Al-Sirah al-Nabawiyyah* (Beirut: Mu'assasah 'Ulum al-Qur'an, 1987), v.3-4, p.413.

[141] Aabadi, Abu Tahir. *Tanwir al-Miqbas min Tafsir ibn Abbas* (Beirut: Dar al-Kutub al-'Ilmiyyah, 1992), pp.549-50.

[142] Muslim, *Sahih Muslim*, hadith 2457; ibn Abi Shaybah, Abu Bakr. *Al-Musannaf* (Riyadh: Dar al-Rushd, 2004), hadith 32335; al-Asbahani, Abu Nu'aym. *Hilyah al-Awliya wa Tabaqat al-Asfiya* (Cairo: Dar al-Khanaji, 2008), v.1, p.150.

[143] Al-Suyuti, *Kitab Raf' Sha'n al-Hubshan*, p.83.

[144] Qawuq, *Hadha Huwa Bilal*, p.137.

[145] Ibid, p.84.

[146] Ibid, p.85.

[147] Ibid, p.195.

[148] See note 47 above.

[149] See note 48 above.

[150] Ibn Hanbal, Ahmad. *Fada'il Sahabah* (Beirut: Dar al-Kutub al-Ilmiyyah, 2008), hadith 1423.

[151] Al-Tabarani, *al-Mu'jam al-Kabir*, hadith 2629.

[152] Ibid, hadith 7288.

[153] Muslim, *Sahih Muslim*, hadith 2457.

[154] See note 48 above.

[155] Al-Suyuti, *Kitab Raf' Sha'n al-Hubshan*, p.61.

[156] Al-'Asqalani, *al-Isabah*, p.83.

[157] Al-Hasani, Abu al-Abbas. *Al-Masabih* (Sana'a: Mu'assasah al-Imam Zayd bin Ali al-Thaqafiyyah, 2002), p.199.

[158] Ibid, p.202.

[159] Al-Suyuti, *Kitab Raf' Sha'n al-Hubshan*, p.63.

[160] Ibid, p.64.

[161] Al-Asbahani, *Ma'rifah al-Sahabah*, p.1036.

[162] Al-'Asqalani, *al-Isabah*, p.1783.

[163] Al-Suyuti, *Kitab Raf' Sha'n al-Hubshan*, p.47.

[164] Ibn Hanbal, *Musnad*, hadith 15327.

[165] See note 162 above.

[166] Al-Shahrudi, Ali. *Mustadrakat 'Ilm Rijal al-Hadith* (Tehran: Husayniyat 'Imad Zadah, 1992), v.8, p.64.

[167] Shams al-Din, Muhammad. *Ansar al-Husayn: Darasah 'an Shuhada Thawrah al-Husayn al-Rijal wa al-Dalalat* (Beirut: Mu'assasah al-Dawliyyah, 1996), pp.80-1.

[168] Ibn al-Jawzi, *Tanwir al-Ghabash*, p.130.

[169] Al-Suyuti, *Kitab Raf' Sha'n al-Hubshan*, p.85.

[170] Al-Zamakhshari, Mahmud. *Tafsir al-Kashshaf 'an Haqa'iq al-Tanzil wa 'Uyun al-Aqawil fi Wujuh al-Ta'wil* (Beirut: Dar al-Ma'rifah, 2005), p.813.

[171] Al-Wahidi, Ali ibn Ahmad. *Asbab al-Nuzul*, trans. Mokrane Guezzou (Amman: Royal Aal al-Bayt Institute for Islamic Thought, 2008), p.177.

[172] See note 48 above.

[173] Ibn Hibban, Abu Hatim. *Tarikh al-Sahabah* (Beirut: Dar al-Kutub al-'Ilmiyyah, 1988), p.49.

[174] Al-Kattani, Muhammad al-Baqir. *Rawqat al-Najjat fi Mawlid Khatim al-Risalat* (Beirut: Dar al-Kutub al-'Ilmiyyah, 2003), p.48.

[175] Ibid, p.54.

[176] Muslim, *Sahih Muslim*, hadith 2453.

[177] Al-Suyuti, *Kitab Raf' Sha'n al-Hubshan*, p.94.

[178] Al-Bahraki, Tayyib. *Hidayah al-Baqi Sharh wa Tahqiq Durar al-Iraqi* (Beirut: Dar al-Kutub al-'Ilmiyyah, 2014), p.54.

[179] See note 177 above.

[180] Ibn al-Jawzi, *Tanwir al-Ghabash*, p.131.

[181] Ibid.

[182] Ibn Kathir states that Ayman was martyred during the Battle of Hunayn. He further states that the following verses were revealed about Ayman and his companions, *"and he who hopes to meet his Lord should do good works, and not associate any other (god) with the worship of his Lord,"* (Q.18:110) Ibn Kathir, Isma'il. *The Life of the Prophet Muhammad* [al-Sira al-Nabawiyya], trans. Trevor Le Gassick (United Kingdom: Garnet Publishing, 2000), vol.4, p.445. Ibn Ishaq stated that at Hunayn many of those who rode with the Prophet ﷺ fled "except that a number of Muhajirs and Ansar and men of his family remained with the apostle. Of the Muhajirs who stood firm were Abu Bakr and Umar; of his family Ali and al-Abbas and Abu Sufyan bin al-Harith and his son; and al-Fadl bin Abbas, and Rabi'a bin al-Harith and Usama bin Zayd and Ayman bin Umm Ayman bin Ubayd who was killed that day". Ibn Hisham, Abu Muhammad. *The Life of Muhammad*, trans. Alfred Guillaume (Oxford: Oxford University Press, 1967), p.569.

[183] See note 178 above.

[184] See note 177 above.

[185] Ibn Hanbal, *Musnad*, hadith 27404.

[186] Al-'Asqalani, *al-Isabah*, p.1944.

[187] Ibid.

[188] Wahidi narrates a more truncated version of this story. He states regarding the verse *"And they give food in spite of love for it to the needy, the orphan, and the captive"* [Q.76:8] that "Ata reported that Ibn Abbas said: 'It happened that Ali ibn Abi Talib hired himself one night to water some palm-trees in exchange for some barley. The following morning, he collected his barley and grinded a third of it out of which they made something to eat, called al-Khazirah. When it was cooked, a poor man came begging from them, and so they gave him the food they had prepared. They then prepared a third of the remaining barley and when it was cooked, an orphan came begging from them, and they gave him the food. They then went and prepared what was left of that barley, but when the food was cooked, a prisoner from among the idolaters came to them and they fed him that food and spent the rest of the day without eating anything. This verse was revealed about this incident'". Al-Wahidi, *Asbab al-Nuzul*, p.245.

[189] Al-Tamimi, al-Nu'man. *Sharh al-Akhbar fi Fa'da'il al-A'immah al-Athar* (Qom: Mu'assasah an-Nashr al-Islami, 2016), v.2, p.328.

[190] Mubarak, Ahmad, and Dawud Walid. *Centering Black Narrative: Black Muslim Nobles Among the Early Pious Muslims* (Rockford: Itrah Press, 2016), pp.52-3. See also Mubarak and Walid, *Centering Black Narrative: Ahl al-Bayt,*

Blackness & Africa, pp.21-3.

[191] Al-Nasiri, Ahmad. *Al-Maraqid al-Islamiyyah fi al-'Alam* (Beirut: Dar al-Hadi, 2006), p.221.

[192] Al-Asbahani, *Ma'rifah al-Sahabah*, pp.277-8.

[193] Ibid, p.943.

[194] Al-'Asqalani, *al-Isabah*, p.367.

[195] Ibid, p.723.

[196] Al-Asbahani, *Ma'rifah al-Sahabah*, p.950; al-'Asqalani, *al-Isabah*, p.366.

[197] Al-Asbahani, *Ma'rifah al-Sahabah*, p.3402.

[198] Ibid.

[199] Al-'Asqalani, *al-Isabah*, p.668.

[200] Al-Asbahani, *Ma'rifah al-Sahabah*, p.1507.

[201] Ibn Hibban, *Tarikh al-Sahabah*, p.190.

[202] Al-Waqidi, Abu Abdullah. *Futuh al-Sham* (Beirut: Dar al-Kutub al-'Ilmiyyah, 2005), v.1, p.156.

[203] Al-Dhahabi, *Siyar A'alam al-Nubala*, v.1, p.297.

[204] Ibn Hisham, *The Life of Muhammad*, p.199; ibn Kathir, *The Life of the Prophet Muhammad*, v.2, p.120.

[205] Ibn Hisham, *The Life of Muhammad*, p.208.

[206] Ibn Hisham, *The Life of Muhammad*, pp.363-4; ibn Kathir, *The Life of the Prophet Muhammad*, v.3, pp.3-4.

[207] Al-Maqrizi, Taqi al-Din. *Kitab al-Mawa'iz wa al-'Itibar bi al-Khutt wa al-Athar li Ma'ruf bi al-Khutt li al-Maqrizi* (Beirut: Dar al-Kutub al-'Ilmiyyah, 1998), v.2, p.76.

[208] Ibn 'Asakir, Ali. *Tahdhib Tarikh bin 'Asakir* (Amman: Dar al-Masirah, 1979), v.7, pp.213-4.

[209] Al-Hakim, *al-Mustadrak 'ala al-Sahihayn*, hadith 5499.

[210] See note 201 above.

[211] Al-'Asqalani, *al-Isabah*, p.488.

[212] Al-'Asqalani, *Fath al-Bari*, v.5, p.216.

[213] Al-Tirmidhi, *Sunan al-Tirmidhi*, hadith 3276; ibn Hanbal, *Musnad*, hadith 25969 & 26508.

[214] Al-Tirmidhi, *Sunan al-Tirmidhi*, hadith 3026; ibn Hanbal, *Musnad*, hadith 13728; al-Tabarani, *al-Mu'jam al-Kabir*, hadith 2671; iIbn Abi Shaybah, *al-Musannaf*, hadith 4739; al-Musuli, Abu Ya'la. *Musnad Abi Ya'la al-Musuli* (Beirut: Dar al-Kutub al-'Ilmiyyah, 1998), hadith 3879; al-Hakim, *al-Mustadrak 'ala al-Sahihayn*, hadith 4763.

[215] Al-Tirmidhi, *Sunan al-Tirmidhi*, hadith 3876; al-Tabarani, *al-Mu'jam al-Kabir*, hadith 4837.

[216] Ibn al-Shajari, *Ma Ittafaq Lafzuhu wa Ikhtilaf Ma'nah*, p.199.

[217] Ibn Hibban, Abu Hatim. *Sahih ibn Hibban* (Beirut: Darl al-Kutub al-'Ilmiyyah, 2014), hadith 6972.

[218] Al-Tirmidhi, *Sunan al-Tirmidhi*, hadith 3789; al-Hakim, *al-Mustadrak 'ala al-Sahihayn*, hadith 4716; al-Tabarani, *al-Mu'jam al-Kabir*, hadith 2638.

[219] Ibn Hanbal, *Musnad*, hadith 26172; al-Nasa'i, Ahmad. *Khasa'is Amir al-Mu'minin 'Ali bin Abi Talib* (Beirut: Dar al-Kitab al-'Arabi, 1996), p.94.

[220] Al-Saqqaf, *Sahih Sharh al-'Aqidah al-Tahawiyyah*, p.651.

[221] Al-Hakim, *al-Mustadrak 'ala al-Sahihayn*, hadith 4717; ibn Hibban, *Sahih ibn Hibban*, hadith 6978.

[222] Al-Bayhaqi, Abu Bakr. *Manaqib al-Shafi'i* (Cairo: Maktabah Dar al-Turath, 1970), v.1, p.63.

[223] Al-Bukhari, *Sahih al-Bukhari*, hadith 3798; Muslim, *Sahih Muslim*, hadith 406; Abu Dawud, *Sunan Abi Dawud*, hadiths 976-978; al-Tirmidhi, *Sunan al-Tirmidhi*, hadith 483; ibn Majah, Abu Abdillah Muhammad ibn Yazid al-Qazwini. *Sunan ibn Majah* (Beirut: Darl al-Kutub al-'Ilmiyyah, 1998), hadith 904.

[224] Al-Ja'fari, Salih. *Al-Qasa'id al-Zaynabiyyat* (Cairo: Dar Jawami' al-Katim, n.d.), p.9.

[225] Al-Jawziyyah, ibn Qayyim. *Jalaa al-Afham fi Fadl al-Salah wa al-Salam 'ala Muhammad Khayr al-Anam* (Riyadh: Dar al-Jawziyyah, 2010), p.354.

[226] Al-Kattani, Muhammad al-Nasir. *'Uyun al-Athar Fima Tawatur al-Ahadith wa al-Akhbar* (Casablanca: Dar al-Hadith al-Kattaniyyah, 1996), p.148.

[227] Al-Haythami, Ali. *Kashf al-Astar 'an Zawa'id al-Bazzar*, (Beirut: Mu'assasah al-Risalah, 2009), p.3322; al-Tabarani, *al-Mu'jam al-Kabir*, hadith 12388.

[228] Al-Hakim, *al-Mustadrak 'ala al-Sahihayn*, hadith 4698; al-Tabarani, *al-Mu'jam al-Kabir*, hadith 6260.

[229] Al-Hakim, *al-Mustadrak 'ala al-Sahihayn*, hadith 4747.

[230] Ibn Hanbal, *Musnad*, hadith 9532; al-Tabarani, *al-Mu'jam al-Kabir*, hadith 2621; ibn Hibban, *Sahih ibn Hibban*, hadith 7103.

[231] Al-Suyuti, Jalal al-Din. *Al-Hawi li al-Fatawa* (Beirut: Dar al-Kitab al-'Arabi, 2014), p.698.

[232] Muslim, *Sahih Muslim*, hadith 2339.

[233] Al-Hakim, Muhammad, and Ahmad al-Ghumari. *Fada'il Fatimah al-Zahra wa ma'ah Risalah fi Tafdil al-Sayyidah Fatimah al-Zahra 'ala Nisa' al-'Alamin* (Tehran: Al-Majma' al-'Alami li Ahl al-Bayt, 2012), p.124.

[234] Ibn al-Jawzi, *Manaqib al-Imam Ahmad*, p.163.

[235] Al-Tabarani, *al-Mu'jam al-Kabir*, hadith 11687.

[236] Al-Tabari, *Tarikh al-Tabari*, p.898.

[237] Ibn al-Jawzi, *Sifat al-Safwah*, p.116; al-Suyuti, Jalal al-Din. *Tarikh al-Khulafa* (Beirut: Dar al-Ma'rifah, 1997), p.150; al-Shablanji, *Nur al-Absar*, p.117.

[238] Al-Ardabili, Abu al-Hasan. *Kashf al-Ghummah fi Ma'rifah al-A'immah* (Beirut: Dar al-Adwa, 1985), v.1, p.74.

[239] Al-Mu'ayyidi, *al-Tuhf Sharh al-Zalaf*, p.24.

[240] Ibn Majah, *Sunan ibn Majah*, hadith 4114.

[241] Al-Tayyibi, 'Ukkashah. *Al-Jifr wa al-Fitan wa Ashrat al-Sa'ah* (Beirut: Dar al-Yusuf, 1999), p.89; al-Suyuti, *al-Hawi li al-Fatawa*, p.480.

[242] Al-Safarini, Muhammad. *Al-Buhur al-Zakharah fi 'Ulum al-Akhirah* (Riyadh: Dar al-'Asimah, 2008), v.1, pp.441-2.

[243] Ibn Rustam, Abu Ja'far. *Dala'il al-A'immah* (Beirut: Mu'assasah al-'Ala, 1988), p.80.

[244] Al-Mu'ayyid, *Tathqif al-Ummah*, p.179.

[245] Ibn al-Jawzi, *Sifat al-Safwah*, p.324.

[246] Al-Samarqandi, Husayn. *Tuhfah al-Talib bi Ma'rifah man Yantasib ila Abdillah wa Abi Talib* (Beirut: Mu'assasah Aal al-Bayt, 2011), p.61.

[247] Al-Kurdi, *al-Intisar li al-Awliya al-Akhyar*, p.337.

[248] Al-Sha'rani, Abd al-Wahhab. *Al-Tabaqat al-Kubra* (Beirut: Dar al-Kutub al-'Ilmiyyah, 2018), p.48.

[249] Al-Shablanji, *Nur al-Absar*, p.212.

[250] Sibt bin al-Jawzi, Yusuf bin Kizoghlu. *Tadhkirah al-Khawass* (Beirut: Dar al-Kutub al-'Ilmiyyah, 2005), p.274.

[251] Ibn al-Jawzi, *Sifat al-Safwah*, p.327.

[252] Ibn al-Jawzi, *Sifat al-Safwah*, p.289.

[253] Sibt bin al-Jawzi, *Tadhkirah al-Khawass*, p.275.

[254] Ibn Husayn, Ali Zayn al-Abidin. *The Psalms of Islam, al-Sahifat al-Kamilat al-Sajjadiyya*, trans. William C. Chittick (London: Muhammadi Trust of Great Britain and Northern Ireland, 1988), p.*x* of foreword.

[255] Abd al-Rahim, Muhammad. *Diwan Zayn al-Abidin* (Damascus: Dar Qutaybah, 2000), pp.71-80.

[256] Ibn al-Jawzi, *Sifat al-Safwah*, pp.325-6.

[257] Al-Shablanji, *Nur al-Absar*, p.217.

[258] Al-Sha'rani, Abd al-Wahab. *Al-Minan al-Kubra* (Beirut: Dar al-Kutub al-'Ilmiyyah, 2010), p.418; Ibrahim, Muhammad. *Maraqid Ahl al-Bayt fi al-Qahirah* (Cairo: Dar al-'Ashirah al-Muhammadiyyah, 2003), p.122.

[259] Baydun, Labib. *Ansab al-'Itrah al-Tahirah* (Beirut: Mu'assasah al-A'alami, 2003), p.81.

[260] Al-'Ubaydi, Asiya. *Aal al-Bayt al-'Alawiyyah fi al-Maghrib wa Atharuhum fi al-Hayat al-'Ammah* (Beirut: Dar al-Kutub al-'Ilmiyyah, 2020), p.59.

[261] See note 248 above.

[262] Ibid.

[263] Ibid.

[264] Ibn Rustam, *Dala'il al-A'immah*, p.94.

[265] Al-Mu'ayyid, *Tathqif al-Ummah*, p.269.

[266] Al-Samarqandi, *Tuhfah al-Talib*, p.46.

[267] Al-Mu'ayyid, *Tathqif al-Ummah*, p.273.

[268] Ibn 'Inabah, *Umdah al-Talib fi Ansab Aal Abi Talib*, p.251.

[269] Al-Shablanji, *Nur al-Absar*, p.318.

[270] Ibn al-Sabbagh, *al-Fusul al-Muhimmah*, p.208.

[271] Sibt bin al-Jawzi, *Tadhkirah al-Khawass*, p.283.

[272] Ibid, p.284.

[273] Ibn 'Inabah, *Umdah al-Talib fi Ansab Aal Abi Talib*, p.251.

[274] Baydun, *Ansab al-'Itrah al-Tahirah*, p.89.

[275] Al-Qummi, *Muntaha al-Amal*, v.2, p.156.

[276] See note 271 above.

[277] Ibn al-Sabbagh, *al-Fusul al-Muhimmah*, p.218.

[278] Al-Haddad, Abdullah. *Al-Da'wah al-Tammah wa al-Tadhkirah al-'Ammah* (Damascus: Dar al-Sanabil, 2017), p.233.

[279] Sibt bin al-Jawzi, *Tadhkirah al-Khawass*, p.284.

[280] Ibid, p.285.

[281] Ibid.

[282] Ibid, p.286.

[283] Alizadeh, Ali Shah. *Tafsir Abi al-Jarudi wa Musnaduh* (Qom: Mu'assasah Dar al-Hadith al-'Ilmiyyah wa al-Thaqafiyyah, 1972), p.341.

[284] Ibid, p.379.

[285] Al-Asbahani, *Tahdhib Hilyah al-Awliya*, v.1, p.507.

[286] Ibid.

[287] Ibid.

[288] Ibid, p.508.

[289] Ibid.

[290] Al-Khawarizmi, Abu al-Mu'ayyid. *Maqtal al-Husayn* (Qom: Dar Anwar al-Huda, 1997), v.2, p.127.

[291] Al-'Ayyashi, Abu al-Nadr. *Tafsir al-'Ayyashi* (Beirut: Mu'assasah al-A'alami, 1991), v.1, p.120.

[292] Al-'Attar, Farid al-Din. *Tadhkirah al-Awliya* (Cairo: Maktabah Afaq, 2015), p.775.

[293] Al-'Ayyashi, *Tafsir al-'Ayyashi*, v.1, p.91.

[294] Al-Mu'ayyid, *Tathqif al-Ummah*, p.288.

[295] Al-Ghurayri, Amir. *Al-Imam Ja'far al-Sadiq wa Ara'uh al-Fiqhiyyah* (Beirut: Dar al-Kutub al-'Ilmiyyah, 2005), p.14.

[296] Ya'qub, Muhammad. *Al-Silsilah al-Dhahabiyyah fi Manaqib al-Sadah al-Naqshabandiyyah* (Damascus: Dar al-Farabi, 2004), p.85.

[297] Al-Ghurayri, *al-Imam Ja'far al-Sadiq wa Ara'uh al-Fiqhiyyah*, p.16.

[298] Al-Zubaydi, Murtada. *Al-Rawd al-Jalli fi Ansab Aal Ba'Alawi* (Damascus: Dar Kinan, 2010), p.22.

[299] Al-Qabbani, 'Adnan. *Al-Futuhat al-Haqqaniyyah fi Manaqib Ujula al-Silsilah al-Dhahabiyyah li al-Tariqah al-Naqshabandiyyah al-'Aliyyah* (Tripoli: Maktabah Ada bwa Fann, 2003), p.112.

[300] Al-Ghurayri, *al-Imam Ja'far al-Sadiq wa Ara'uh al-Fiqhiyyah*, pp.23-4.

[301] Ibid, p.25.

[302] Al-Shablanji, *Nur al-Absar*, p.300.

[303] Sibt bin al-Jawzi, *Tadhkirah al-Khawass*, pp.282-3.

[304] Ya'qub, *al-Silsilah al-Dhahabiyyah*, p.91-3.

[305] Ibn al-Sabbagh, *al-Fusul al-Muhimmah*, p.227.

[306] Ya'qub, *al-Silsilah al-Dhahabiyyah*, p.93.

[307] Ibn Majid, Abd al-Rahman. *Ansab al-Talibin wa al-'Alawiyyin al-Qadimiyyin wa Nabdhah min Akhbarihim* (Cairo: Wazarah al-Thaqafi, 2002), p.43.

[308] Al-'Attar, *Tadhkirah al-Awliya*, p.155.

[309] Al-Khalili, Muhammad. *Min Amali al-Imam al-Sadiq wa Huwa Sharh ma Umalah al-Imam 'ala Talmidhih al-Mufaddil bin 'Umar al-Ju'fi* (Beirut: Mu'assasah al-'Ala, 1984), v.2, p.12.

[310] Zay'ur, Ali. *Kamil al-Tafsir al-Sufi al-'Irfani li al-Qur'an 'inda al-Sadiq* (Beirut: Maktabah al-Shawq, 2002), p.81.

[311] Ibid, p.94.

[312] Ibid, p.143.

[313] Al-Khalili, *Min Amali al-Imam al-Sadiq*, v.2, p.21.

[314] Al-Tha'labi, Ahmad. *Ahl al-Bayt fi Tafsir al-Tha'labi* (Qom: Markaz al-Buhuth wa al-Darasat Ma'ahd al-Qur'an al-Karim, 1962), p.166.

[315] Al-Saqqaf, Hadi. *Al-Jawahar Al-Masun fi Rawayah Qalun* (Beirut: Dar al-Hawi, 1997), p.176.

[316] Al-Tha'labi, Ahmad. *Ahl al-Bayt fi Tafsir al-Tha'labi* (Qom: Markaz al-Buhuth wa al-Darasat Ma'ahd al-Qur'an al-Karim, 1962), p.57.

[317] Ibn Muhammad al-Baqir, Ja'far al-Sadiq. *Misbah al-Shari'ah* (Beirut: Mu'assasah al-A'alami, 1992), p.13.

[318] Al-Ghurayri, *al-Imam Ja'far al-Sadiq wa Ara'uh al-Fiqhiyyah*, p.36.

[319] al-Dhahabi, *Siyar A'alam al-Nubala*, v.6, p.261.

[320] Al-Asbahani, *Tahdhib Hilyah al-Awliya*, v.1, p.512.

[321] Al-Asbahani, al-Raghib. *Arwa ma Qil al-Shaja'ah wa al-Jubn wa al-Hamm wa al-Amal* (Beirut: 'Alam al-Kutub, 1999), p.40.

[322] Al-Harani, al-Hasan. *Tuhuf al-'Uqul 'an Aal al-Rasul* (Cairo: Dar al-Kitab al-'Arabi, 2014), p.388.

[323] Al-Ardabili, Ahmad. *Al-Futuwwa* (Amman: Dar al-Razi, 2003), p.10.

[324] Al-'Attar, *Tadhkirah al-Awliya*, p.154.

[325] Al-Sha'rani, *al-Tabaqat al-Kubra*, p.50.

[326] Ibid.

[327] Al-Tabarsi, Hasan. *Makarim al-Akhlaq* (Beirut: Mu'assasah al-A'alami, 2009), p.110.

[328] Al-Asbahani, *Tahdhib Hilyah al-Awliya*, v.1, p.513.

[329] Ibn al-Sabbagh, *al-Fusul al-Muhimmah*, p.226.

[330] Al-Tabarsi, *Makarim al-Akhlaq*, p.192.

[331] Zay'ur, *Kamil al-Tafsir al-Sufi al-'Irfani li al-Qur'an 'inda al-Sadiq*, p.76.

[332] Al-Nasiri, *al-Maraqid al-Islamiyyah fi al-'Alam*, p.153.

[333] Al-Bukhari, Sahl. *Sirr al-'Alawiyyah fi Ansab al-Sadah al-'Alawiyyah* (Qom: Maktabah Ayatillah al-'Uzma al-Mara'shi al-Najafi, 2011), p.65.

[334] Al-Asbahani, *Maqatil al-Talibin*, p.343.

[335] Ibid, p.345.

[336] Al-Shablanji, *Nur al-Absar*, pp.300-1.

[337] Al-Samarqandi, *Tuhfah al-Talib*, p.112.

[338] See note 332 above.

[339] See note 337 above.

[340] Al-Hasani, *al-Masabih*, p.424.

[341] Al-'Aqiqi, Yahya. *Kitab al-Mu'qibin min Walad al-Imam Abi al-Hasan Ali bin Abi Talib* (Amman: Urwiqah li al-Darasat, 2010), p.237; al-Asbahani, *Maqatil al-Talibin*, p.206.

[342] Al-Tabari, *Tarikh al-Tabari*, p.1528; al-Mu'ayyidi, *al-Tuhf Sharh al-Zalaf*, p.52.

[343] Ibn 'Inabah, *Umdah al-Talib fi Ansab Aal Abi Talib*, p.121.

[344] Al-Mu'ayyidi, *al-Tuhf Sharh al-Zalaf*, pp.52-3.

[345] Al-Asbahani, *Maqatil al-Talibin*, p.207.

[346] Al-Mu'ayyidi, *al-Tuhf Sharh al-Zalaf*, pp.54-5.

[347] Al-Asbahani, *Maqatil al-Talibin*, p.171.

[348] Ibid, p.162.

[349] Ibid, p.180.

[350] Ibid, p.244.

[351] Al-Suyuti, *Tarikh al-Khulafa*, pp.230-1; ibn 'Inabah, *Umdah al-Talib fi Ansab*

Aal Abi Talib, p.123.

[352] Al-Hasani, *al-Masabih*, p.333.

[353] Al-'Ubaydi, *Aal al-Bayt al-'Alawiyyah fi al-Maghrib*, p.53.

[354] Al-Mu'ayyid, *Tathqif al-Ummah*, p.307.

[355] Al-Samarqandi, *Tuhfah al-Talib*, p.102.

[356] Al-Himsayyi, Mustafa. *Hayat Nisa min Bani Hashim* (Beirut: Dar al-Mahajjah al-Bayda, 2009), p.324.

[357] Al-Sha'rani, *al-Tabaqat al-Kubra*, p.98.

[358] Al-'Aqiqi, *Kitab al-Mu'qibin*, p.334.

[359] Al-Shablanji, *Nur al-Absar*, p.287.

[360] Al-Zubaydi, *al-Rawd al-Jalli fi Ansab Aal Ba'Alawi*, p.21.

[361] Al-Himsayyi, *Hayat Nisa min Bani Hashim*, p.222.

[362] Al-Nasiri, *al-Maraqid al-Islamiyyah fi al-'Alam*, p.240.

[363] Ibn al-Sabbagh, *al-Fusul al-Muhimmah*, p.229.

[364] Ibn 'Inabah, *Umdah al-Talib fi Ansab Aal Abi Talib*, p.253.

[365] Al-'Asqalani, ibn Hajar. *Tahdhib al-Tahdhib* (Beirut: Mu'assasah al-Risalah, 2008), v.3, p.173.

[366] Al-Mu'ayyidi, Muhammad. *Zubad al-Ad'iyyah* (Sa'dah: Mu'assasah al-Mustafa al-Thaqafiyyah, 2003), pp.90-5.

[367] Ibn Shahrashub, Abu Ja'far. *Manaqib Aal Abi Talib* (Beirut: Mu'assasah al-A'alami, 2009), v.4, p.633.

[368] Al-Sha'rani, *al-Tabaqat al-Kubra*, p.57.

[369] Al-Shablanji, *Nur al-Absar*, pp.287-8; al-Sha'rani, *al-Tabaqat al-Kubra*, p.96; al-Sakhawi, Ali. *Tuhfah al-Ahbab wa Bughyah al-Tullab* (Cairo: Dar al-Muqattam, 2010), p.102.

[370] See note 298 above.

[371] Al-Asbahani, *Maqatil al-Talibin*, p.440.

[372] Ibn 'Inabah, *Umdah al-Talib fi Ansab Aal Abi Talib*, p.259.

[373] Ibn Majid, *Ansab al-Talibin*, p.60.

[374] Al-Damiri, Kamal al-Din. *Hayat al-Hayawan al-Kubra* (Beirut: Dar al-Kutub al-'Ilmiyyah, 2007), v.1, p.432.

[375] Ibn al-Sabbagh, *al-Fusul al-Muhimmah*, p.235.

[376] Ibn Ja'far al-Sadiq, Ali. *Masa'il Ali bin Ja'far wa Mustadrakatuha* (Beirut: Mu'assasah Aal al-Bayt li Ihya al-Turath, 2010), p.349.

[377] Al-Harani, *Tuhuf al-'Uqul 'an Aal al-Rasul*, p.417.

[378] Ibid, p.420.

[379] Ibid, p.423.

[380] Ibid, p.427.

[381] Ibid, p.428.

[382] Ibid, p.435.

[383] Ibid, p.446.

[384] Al-Asbahani, *Maqatil al-Talibin*, p.333.

[385] Ibn 'Inabah, *Umdah al-Talib fi Ansab Aal Abi Talib*, p.133.

[386] Al-Dhahabi, Shams al-Din. *Mizan al-'Itidal fi Naqd al-Rijal* (Riyadh: Dar al-Ma'rifah, 2009), v.4, p.404.

[387] Al-Zu'bi, *Ithaf al-Akabir fi Sirah wa Manaqib al-Imam Muhyi al-Din Abd al-Qadir al-Jiylani*, p.131.

[388] Al-Nasiri, *al-Maraqid al-Islamiyyah fi al-'Alam*, p.184.

[389] Ibn 'Inabah, *Umdah al-Talib fi Ansab Aal Abi Talib*, p.133.

[390] Al-'Ubaydi, *Aal al-Bayt al-'Alawiyyah fi al-Maghrib*, pp.54-5.

[391] Al-Zu'bi, *Ithaf al-Akabir fi Sirah wa Manaqib al-Imam Muhyi al-Din Abd al-Qadir al-Jiylani*, p.134.

[392] Ibn 'Inabah, *Umdah al-Talib fi Ansab Aal Abi Talib*, p.135.

[393] Al-Haruni, Yahya. *Al-Ifadah fi Tarikh al-A'immah al-Sadah* (Tehran: Mirath Maktub, 1967), p.28.

[394] Ibid.

[395] Al-Razi, Ahmad. *Akhbar Fakhkh wa Khabr Yahya bin Abdillah wa Akhih Idris bin Abdillah* (Tunis: Dar al-Gharb al-Islami, 2011), p.61.

[396] Al-Haruni, Jamal al-Din. *Hidyah al-Raghibin ila Madhhab al-'Itrah al-Tayyibin* (Beirut: Dar al-Kutub al-'Ilmiyya, 2007), p.104.

[397] Al-Baqa'i, Iman. *Diwan al-Imam al-Shafi'i* (Beirut: Dar al-A'alami, 2000), p.91.

[398] Nasrullah, Sa'd. *Dawlah al-Adarisah fi al-Maghrib al-'Asr al-Dhahabiyyah* (Beirut: Dar al-Nahdah al-'Arabiyyah, 1996), v.2, p.106; ibn Abd al-Salam, al-Tahir. *Hisn al-Salam Bayna Yaday Awlad Mawlay Abd al-Salam* (Casablanca: Dar al-Thaqafah, 1978), p.276.

[399] Al-'Ubaydi, *Aal al-Bayt al-'Alawiyyah fi al-Maghrib*, p.71.

[400] Al-Mu'ayyidi, *al-Tuhf Sharh al-Zalaf*, p.75.

[401] Al-Salawi, *al-Istiqsa*, v.1, p.138; ibn Abd al-Salam, *Hisn al-Salam*, p.276.

[402] Al-'Ubaydi, *Aal al-Bayt al-'Alawiyyah fi al-Maghrib*, p.32.

[403] Ibid, pp.37-8.

[404] Al-Mu'ayyid, *Tathqif al-Ummah*, p.316.

[405] Ibid, p.319.

[406] Al-Mu'ayyidi, *al-Tuhf Sharh al-Zalaf*, p.85.

[407] Al-Mu'ayyid, *Tathqif al-Ummah*, p.318.

[408] See note 406 above.

[409] Al-Mu'ayyid, *Tathqif al-Ummah*, p.317.

[410] See note 406 above.

[411] Al-Mu'ayyid, *Tathqif al-Ummah*, p.319.

[412] Al-Barr, Muhammad. *Al-Imam Ali al-Rida wa Risalah fi al-Tibb al-Nabawi* (Beirut: Dar al-Manahil, 2010), p.97; al-Ghazali, Abu Hamid. *Ihya al-'Ulum al-Din* (Beirut: Dar al-Kutub al-'Ilmiyyah, 2002), v.3, p.64.

[413] Al-Musawi, Mahdi. *Al-Mu'qibun min Aal Abi Talib* (Qom: Mu'assasah 'Ashura, 2016), v.2, p.21; al-Shablanji, *Nur al-Absar*, p.232.

[414] Al-Wasiti, Sharif al-Din. *Al-Burhan al-Mu'ayyid li Sahib Madd al-Yad Mawlana al-Ghawt Al-Sharif al-Rifa'i Ahmad* (Beirut: Dar al-Kutub al-'Ilmiyyah, 2010), p.21.

[415] Al-Daylami, Abu Shuja'. *Musnad al-Firdaws bi Ma'thur al-Khatab* (Beirut: Dar al-Kutub al-'Ilmiyyah, 2010), v.5, p.251; al-Rifa'i, Ahmad. *Al-Rifa'i, Halah Ahl al-Haqiqah ma'a Allah Taa'la* (Beirut: Dar al-Kutub al-'Ilmiyyah, 2010), p.127.

[416] Ibn Musa al-Kazim, Ali al-Rida. *Sahifah al-Imam al-Rida* (Qom: Mu'assasah al-Imam al-Mahdi, 1987), hadith 1; ibn Babawayh, Abu Ja'far. *'Uyun al-Akhbar al-Rida* (Beirut: Mu'assasah al-A'alami, 1984), v.1, p.144.

[417] Sibt bin al-Jawzi, *Tadhkirah al-Khawass*, p.295; ibn al-Sabbagh, *al-Fusul al-Muhimmah*, p.251.

[418] Al-Kurdi, *al-Intisar li al-Awliya al-Akhyar*, p.345.

[419] Al-Barr, *al-Imam Ali al-Rida*, pp.138-9.

[420] Al-Ghazali, *Ihya al-'Ulum al-Din*, v.3, p.65.

[421] Al-Qummi, *Muntaha al-Amal*, v.2, p.368.

[422] Ibid, p.371.

[423] Al-Asbahani, *Maqatil al-Talibin*, p.470.

[424] Al-'Asqalani, *Tahdhib al-Tahdhib*, v.7, p.339.

[425] Ibn 'Inabah, *Umdah al-Talib fi Ansab Aal Abi Talib*, p.226; ibn al-Sabbagh, *al-Fusul al-Muhimmah*, p.242.

[426] Al-Himsayyi, *Hayat Nisa min Bani Hashim*, p.232.

[427] Al-Jazari, Shams al-Din. *Asma al-Manaqib fi Tadhhib Asna al-Matalib fi Manaqib al-Imam Amir al-Mu'minin Ali ibn Abi Talib* (Beirut: Dar al-Kutub al-'Ilmiyyah. 2005), pp.32-3.

[428] Al-Nasiri, *al-Maraqid al-Islamiyyah fi al-'Alam*, p.30.

[429] Ibn Majid, *Ansab al-Talibin*, p.65.

[430] Ibn al-Sabbagh, *al-Fusul al-Muhimmah*, p.248.

[431] Al-Harani, *Tuhuf al-'Uqul 'an Aal al-Rasul*, p.475.

[432] Ibid.

[433] Ibid.

[434] Ibid, p.476.

[435] Ibid.

[436] Ibn al-Sabbagh, *al-Fusul al-Muhimmah*, p.252; al-Mu'ayyid, *Tathqif al-Ummah*, pp.439-440; al-Qummi, *Muntaha al-Amal*, v.2, p.419.

[437] Al-Nu'man, Muhammad. *Kitab al-Irshad* (Beirut: Mu'assasah al-A'alami, 2008), p.399.

[438] Ibn Rustam, *Dala'il al-A'immah*, p.197.

[439] Ibn Taymiyyah, Taqi al-Din. *Majmu'a Fatawa Shaykh al-Islam bin Taymiyyah* (Beirut: Dar al-Kutub al-'Ilmiyyah, 2015), v.4, p.487.

[440] Al-Razi, Fakhr al-Din. *Al-Shajarah al-Mubarakah fi Ansab al-Talibyyah* (Qom: Maktabah Ayatillah al-'Uzma al-Mar'ashi al-Najafi, 1998), p.91.

[441] Al-Qummi, *Muntaha al-Amal*, v.2, pp.434-5.

[442] Al-Nasiri, *al-Maraqid al-Islamiyyah fi al-'Alam*, p.77.

[443] Ibn al-Sabbagh, *al-Fusul al-Muhimmah*, p.269.

[444] Ibid.

[445] Ibid, p.270.

[446] Ibid.

[447] Ibid, p.271.

[448] Ibid.

[449] Ibid.

[450] Al-Ardabili, *Kashf al-Ghummah*, v.3, p.166.

[451] Al-Shablanji, *Nur al-Absar*, p.251.

[452] See note 450 above.

[453] Al-Mu'ayyid, *Tathqif al-Ummah*, p.466.

[454] Ibn al-Sabbagh, *al-Fusul al-Muhimmah*, p.279.

[455] See note 442 above.

[456] Al-Kurdi, *al-Intisar li al-Awliya al-Akhyar*, p.494.

[457] Al-Harani, *Tuhuf al-'Uqul 'an Aal al-Rasul*, p.518.

[458] Ibn Rustam, *Dala'il al-A'immah*, p.219; al-Samarqandi, *Tuhfah al-Talib*, p.62.

[459] Sibt bin al-Jawzi, *Tadhkirah al-Khawass*, p.303.

[460] Al-Mu'ayyid, *Tathqif al-Ummah*, p.492.

[461] Al-Haydari, Muhammad. *Al-Durar al-Bahiyyah fi al-Ansab al-Haydayriyyah wa al-Uwaysiyyah* (Aleppo: Maktabah Dar al-Falah, 1985), p.73.

[462] Ibn 'Inabah, *Umdah al-Talib fi Ansab Aal Abi Talib*, p.256.

[463] Sibt bin al-Jawzi, *Tadhkirah al-Khawass*, p.304.

[464] Al-Shablanji, *Nur al-Absar*, p.254.

[465] Al-Samarqandi, *Tuhfah al-Talib*, p.63.

[466] Al-Shablanji, *Nur al-Absar*, p.257.

[467] Ibn 'Arabi, Muhyi al-Din. *Futuh al-Makkiyyah fi Ma'rifah al-Asrar al-*

Malikiyyah wa al-Mulkiyyah (Beirut: Dar Ihya al-Turath al-'Arabi, 1997), v.3, p.319.

[468] Al-Balkhi, Abu al-Qasim. *Kitab al-Maqalat wa ma'ah 'Uyun al-Masa'il wa al-Jawabat* (Istanbul: Kuramer Center for Qur'anic Studies, 2018), p.88.

[469] Al-Jushami, al-Muhsin. *'Uyun al-Masa'il fi al-Usul* (Istanbul: Dar al-Ihsan, 2018), p.82.

[470] Ibn 'Inabah, *Umdah al-Talib fi Ansab Aal Abi Talib*, pp.256-7.

[471] Al-Samarqandi, *Tuhfah al-Talib*, p.93.

[472] Al-Jushami, al-Hakim. *Jalaa al-Absar* (Collection of Maktabah Jami' al-Kabir, Sana'a), p.104.

[473] Ibn al-Sabbagh, *al-Fusul al-Muhimmah*, p.281.

[474] Al-Harani, *Tuhuf al-'Uqul 'an Aal al-Rasul*, p.521.

[475] Ibid, p.523.

[476] Ibid, p.524.

[477] Ibid.

[478] Ibid, p.525.

[479] Ibid, p.550.

[480] Al-Mu'ayyidi, Majd al-Din. *Al-Masabih* (Amman: Mu'assasah al-Imam Zayd bin 'Ali al-Thaqafiyyah, 2002), p.602.

[481] Al-Mu'ayyidi, *al-Tuhf Sharh al-Zalaf*, p.114.

[482] Ibn al-Athir, Ali. *Al-Kamil fi al-Tarikh* (Beirut: Dar al-Kutub al-'Ilmiyyah, 2008), v.6, p.144.

[483] Al-Mu'ayyidi, *al-Tuhf Sharh al-Zalaf*, p.115.

[484] Ahmad, Mujtaba. *Nafa'is al-Ta'wil* (Beirut: Maktabah al-'Aalami, 2010), v.1, p.395.

[485] Madelung, Wilferd. *Akhbar A'immah al-Zaydiyyah fi Tabaristan wa Dalaman wa Jiylan* (Beirut: Orient-Istitut der Deutschen Morgenlandischen Gesellschaft, 1987), p.71.

[486] See note 480 above.

[487] Ibn Husayn, Sharif al-Murtada, Ali. *Masa'il al-Nasiriyyat* (Tehran: Rabatah al-Thaqafah wa al-'Alaqat al-Islamiyyah, 1997), p.120.

[488] Ibid, p.143.

[489] Ibid, p.179.

[490] Ibid, p.180.

[491] Ibid, p.182

[492] Ibid, p.197.

[493] Ibid, p.221.

[494] Ibid, p.228.

[495] Ibid, p.230.

[496] Ibid, p.234.

[497] Ibid, p.242.

[498] Ibid, p.244.

[499] Ibid, p.256.

[500] Ibid, p.299.

[501] Ibid, p.330.

[502] Ibn 'Inabah, *Umdah al-Talib fi Ansab Aal Abi Talib*, p.259.

[503] Al-Mu'ayyid, *Tathqif al-Ummah*, p.345.

[504] Ibn al-Qasim, Ibrahim. *Tabaqat al-Zaydiyyah al-Kubra* (Amman: Mu'assasah al-Imam Zayd bin Ali al-Thaqafiyyah, 2001), v.1, p.960.

Bibliography

Published Sources

Aabadi, Abu Tahir. *Tanwir al-Miqbas min Tafsir ibn Abbas* (Beirut: Dar al-Kutub al-'Ilmiyyah, 1992).

Abbad, Isma'il. *Al-Muhit fi al-Lughah* (Qom: 'Alam al-Kutub, 1972).

Abd al-Rahim, Muhammad. *Diwan Zayn al-Abidin* (Damascus: Dar Qutaybah, 2000).

Ibn Abi Shaybah, Abu Bakr. *Al-Musannaf* (Riyadh: Dar al-Rushd, 2004).

Ibn Abd al-Barr, Yusuf. *Al-Tamhid Lamma fi al-Muwatta' min al-Ma'ani wa al-Masanid* (Beirut: Dar al-Kutub al-'Ilmiyyah, 2010).

Ibn Abd al-Salam, al-Tahir. *Hisn al-Salam Bayna Yaday Awlad Mawlay Abd al-Salam* (Casablanca: Dar al-Thaqafah, 1978).

Ibn 'Adi, Abu Ahmad. *Al-Kamil fi Du'afa al-Rijal* (Riyadh: Maktabah al-Rushd, 2013).

Ahmad, Mujtaba. *Nafa'is al-Ta'wil* (Beirut: Maktabah al-'Aalami, 2010).

Albani, Muhammad. *Silsilah al-Ahadith al-Da'ifah wa al-Mawdu'ah* (Cairo: Dar al-Ma'arif, 2008).

Ali, Abdullah. *The 'Negro' in Arab-Muslim Consciousness* (Milpitas: Claritas Books, 2018).

Al-Ali, Salih. *Sahib al-Zanj wa Dawlatih al-Mahzuzah* (Beirut: Dar al-Madar al-Islami, 2006)

Ibn al-Athir, Ali. *Al-Kamil fi al-Tarikh* (Beirut: Dar al-Kutub al-'Ilmiyyah, 2008).

Alizadeh, Ali Shah. *Tafsir Abi al-Jarudi wa Musnaduh* (Qom: Mu'assasah Dar al-Hadith al-'Ilmiyyah wa al-Thaqafiyyah, 1972).

Ibn Ali, Zayd. *Musnad al-Imam Zayd* (Beirut: Darl al-Kutub al-'Ilmiyyah, 1999).

Al-'Aqiqi, Yahya. *Kitab al-Mu'qibin min Walad al-Imam Abi al-Hasan Ali bin Abi Talib* (Amman: Urwiqah li al-Darasat, 2010).

Ibn 'Arabi, Muhyi al-Din. *Futuh al-Makkiyyah fi Ma'rifah al-Asrar al-Malikiyyah wa al-Mulkiyyah* (Beirut: Dar Ihya al-Turath al-'Arabi, 1997).

Al-Ardabili, Abu al-Hasan. *Kashf al-Ghummah fi Ma'rifah al-A'immah* (Beirut: Dar al-Adwa, 1985).

Al-Ardabili, Ahmad. *Al-Futuwwa* (Amman: Dar al-Razi, 2003).

Ibn 'Asakir, Ali. *Tahdhib Tarikh bin 'Asakir* (Amman: Dar al-Masirah, 1979).

Al-Asbahani, Abu al-Faraj. *Maqatil al-Talibin* (Beirut: Mu'assasah al-A'alami, 2007).

Al-Asbahani, Abu Nu'aym. *Hilyah al-Awliya wa Tabaqat al-Asfiya* (Cairo: Dar al-Khanaji, 2008).

—. *Ma'rifah al-Sahabah* (Riyadh: Dar al-Watan, 1998).

—. *Tahdhib Hilyah al-Awliya wa Tabaqat al-Asfiya* (Beirut: Al-Maktabah al-Islami, 1998).

Al-Asbahani, al-Raghib. *Arwa ma Qil al-Shaja'ah wa al-Jubn wa al-Hamm wa al-Amal* (Beirut: 'Alam al-Kutub, 1999).

Al-'Asqalani, ibn Hajar. *Al-Isabah fi Tamyiz al-Sahabah* (Beirut: Maktabah al-'Asriyyah, 2012).

—. *Fath al-Bari Sharh Sahih al-Bukhari* (Cairo: Dar al-Salafiyyah, 2015).

—. *Lisan al-Mizan* (Beruit: Dar al-Basha'ir al-Islamiyyah, 2002).

—. *Tahdhib al-Tahdhib* (Beirut: Mu'assasah al-Risalah, 2008).

Al-'Attar, Farid al-Din. *Tadhkirah al-Awliya* (Cairo: Maktabah Afaq, 2015).

Al-'Ayashi, Ahmad. *Kashf al-Hijab 'Aman Talaqa ma'a al-Shaykh al-Tijani min al-Ashab* (Beirut: Al-Maktabah al-Sha'biyyah, n.d.).

Al-'Ayyashi, Abu al-Nadr. *Tafsir al-'Ayyashi* (Beirut: Mu'assasah al-A'alami, 1991).

Ibn Babawayh, Abu Ja'far. *Ilal al-Shara'i* (Beirut: Mu'assasah al-A'alami, 2007).

—. *'Uyun al-Akhbar al-Rida* (Beirut: Mu'assasah al-A'alami, 1984).

Al-Bahraki, Tayyib. *Hidayah al-Baqi Sharh wa Tahqiq Durar al-Iraqi* (Beirut: Dar al-Kutub al-'Ilmiyyah, 2014).

Al-Baladhuri, Ahmad. *Ansab al-Ashraf* (Beirut: Dar al-Fikr, 1996).

Al-Balkhi, Abu al-Qasim. *Kitab al-Maqalat wa ma'ah 'Uyun al-Masa'il wa al-Jawabat* (Istanbul: Kuramer Center for Qur'anic Studies, 2018).

Al-Baqa'i, Iman. *Diwan al-Imam al-Shafi'i* (Beirut: Dar al-A'alami, 2000).

Al-Barr, Muhammad. *Al-Imam Ali al-Rida wa Risalah fi al-Tibb al-Nabawi* (Beirut: Dar al-Manahil, 2010).

Baydun, Labib. *Ansab al-'Itrah al-Tahirah* (Beirut: Mu'assasah al-A'alami, 2003).

Al-Bayhaqi, Abu Bakr. *Al-Asma wa al-Siffat* (Cairo: Maktabah al-Taw'iyyah al-Islamiyyah, 2009).

—. *Al-Sunan al-Kubra* (Beirut: Dar al-Kutub al-'Ilmiyyah, 2008).

—. *Manaqib al-Shafi'i* (Cairo: Maktabah Dar al-Turath, 1970).

—. *Shu'b al-Iman* (Beirut: Dar al-Kutub al-'Ilmiyyah, 2008).

Al-Bukhari, Muhammad. *Sahih al-Bukhari* (Riyadh: Dar ibn Hazm, 2015).

Al-Bukhari, Sahl. *Sirr al-'Alawiyyah fi Ansab al-Sadah al-'Alawiyyah* (Qom: Maktabah Ayatillah al-'Uzma al-Mara'shi al-Najafi, 2011).

Al-Damiri, Kamal al-Din. *Hayat al-Hayawan al-Kubra* (Beirut: Dar al-Kutub al-'Ilmiyyah, 2007).

Al-Daylami, Abu al-Fath. *Kitab al-Burhan fi Tafsir al-Qur'an* (Qom: Mu'assasah al-Ba'thah, 2000).

Al-Daylami, Abu Shuja'. *Musnad al-Firdaws bi Ma'thur al-Khatab* (Beirut: Dar al-Kutub al-'Ilmiyyah, 2010).

Al-Dhahabi, Shams al-Din. *Al-Isra'iliyyat fi al-Tafsir wa al-Hadith* (Cairo: Maktabah Wahbah, 1990).

—. *Mizan al-'Itidal fi Naqd al-Rijal* (Riyadh: Dar al-Ma'rifah, 2009).

—. *Siyar A'alam al-Nubala* (Beirut: Mu'assasah al-Risalah, 2015).

—. *Tartib al-Mawdu'at* (Beirut: Dar al-Kutub al-'Ilmiyyah, 2009).

Al-Ghazali, Abu Hamid. *Ihya al-'Ulum al-Din* (Beirut: Dar al-Kutub al-'Ilmiyyah, 2002).

Al-Ghurayri, Amir. *Al-Imam Ja'far al-Sadiq wa Ara'uh al-Fiqhiyyah* (Beirut: Dar al-Kutub al-'Ilmiyyah, 2005).

Al-Haddad, Abdullah. *Al-Da'wah al-Tammah wa al-Tadhkirah al-'Ammah* (Damascus: Dar al-Sanabil, 2017).

Al-Hakim, Muhammad. *Al-Mustadrak 'ala al-Sahihayn* (Beirut: Dar al-Kutub al-'Ilmiyyah, 2011).

Al-Hakim, Muhammad, and Ahmad al-Ghumari. *Fada'il Fatimah al-Zahra wa ma'ah Risalah fi Tafdil al-Sayyidah Fatimah al-Zahra 'ala Nisa' al-'Alamin* (Tehran: Al-Majma' al-'Alami li Ahl al-Bayt, 2012).

Ibn Hanbal, Ahmad. *Fada'il Sahabah* (Beirut: Dar al-Kutub al-Ilmiyyah, 2008).

—. *Musnad al-Imam Ahmad bin Hanbal* (Beirut: Mu'assasah al-Risalah, 2001).

Ibn Hani, Ishaq. *Masa'il al-Imam Ahmad bin Hanbal Rawayah li Ishaq bin Ibrahim bin Hani al-Niysaburi* (Cairo: Dar al-Mawaddah, 2008).

Al-Harani, al-Hasan. *Tuhuf al-'Uqul 'an Aal al-Rasul* (Cairo: Dar al-Kitab al-'Arabi, 2014).

Al-Haruni, Jamal al-Din. *Hidyah al-Raghibin ila Madhhab al-'Itrah al-Tayyibin* (Beirut: Dar al-Kutub al-'Ilmiyya, 2007).

Al-Haruni, Yahya. *Al-Ifadah fi Tarikh al-A'immah al-Sadah* (Tehran: Mirath Maktub, 1967).

Al-Hasani, Abu al-Abbas. *Al-Masabih* (Sana'a: Mu'assasah al-Imam Zayd bin Ali al-Thaqafiyyah, 2002).

Al-Haydari, Muhammad. *Al-Durar al-Bahiyyah fi al-Ansab al-Haydayriyyah wa al-Uwaysiyyah* (Aleppo: Maktabah Dar al-Falah, 1985).

Al-Haythami, Ali. *Kashf al-Astar 'an Zawa'id al-Bazzar* (Beirut: Mu'assasah al-Risalah, 2009).

Ibn Hibban, Abu Hatim. *Al-Mujrihin min al-Muhaddithin* (Riyadh: Dar al-Sumayi', 2009).

—. *Sahih ibn Hibban* (Beirut: Darl al-Kutub al-'Ilmiyyah, 2014).

—. *Tarikh al-Sahabah* (Beirut: Dar al-Kutub al-'Ilmiyyah, 1988).

Al-Himsayyi, Mustafa. *Hayat Nisa min Bani Hashim* (Beirut: Dar al-Mahajjah al-Bayda, 2009).

Ibn Hisham, Abu Muhammad. *Al-Sirah al-Nabawiyyah* (Beirut: Mu'assasah 'Ulum al-Qur'an, 1987).

—. *The Life of Muhammad*, trans. Alfred Guillaume (Oxford: Oxford University Press, 1967).

Ibn Husayn, Ali Zayn al-Abidin. *Al-Sahifah al-Sajjadiyyah al-Kamilah* (Baghdad: Maktab Dar al-Kutub al-'Iraqiyyah, 2012).

—. *The Psalms of Islam, al-Sahifat al-kamilat al-sajjadiyya*, trans. William C. Chittick (London: Muhammadi Trust of Great Britain and Northern Ireland, 1988).

Ibn Husayn, Sharif al-Murtada, Ali. *Masa'il al-Nasiriyyat* (Tehran: Rabatah al-Thaqafah wa al-'Alaqat al-Islamiyyah, 1997).

Ibrahim, Muhammad. *Maraqid Ahl al-Bayt fi al-Qahirah* (Cairo: Dar al-'Ashirah al-Muhammadiyyah, 2003)

Ibn 'Inabah, Ahmad. *Umdah al-Talib fi Ansab Aal Abi Talib*

(Beirut: Mu'assasah al-'Ala, 2015).

'Izzan, Muhammad. *Majmu' Kutub wa Rasa'il al-Imam Zayd bin Ali* (Sana'a: Dar al-Hikmah al-Yamaniyyah, 2001).

Ibn Ja'far al-Sadiq, Ali. *Masa'il Ali bin Ja'far wa Mustadrakatuha* (Beirut: Mu'assasah Aal al-Bayt li Ihya al-Turath, 2010).

Al-Ja'fari, Salih. *Al-Qasa'id al-Zaynabiyyat* (Cairo: Dar Jawami' al-Katim, n.d.).

Al-Jahiz, Abu Uthman. *Rasa'il al-Jahiz* (Beirut: Dar al-Kutub al-'Ilmiyyah, 2013).

Ibn al-Jawzi, Abu al-Faraj. *Kitab al-Mawdu'at* (Madinah: Maktabah al-Salafiyyah, 1966).

——. *Majalis ibn al-Jawzi fi al-Mutashabihah min al-Ayat al-Qur'aniyyah* (Beirut: Darl al-Kutub al-'Ilmiyyah, 2013).

——. *Manaqib al-Imam Ahmad* (Cairo: Dar Hijr, 2008).

——. *Tanwir al-Ghabash fi Fadl al-Sudan wa al-Habash* (Riyadh: Dar al-Sharif, 2010).

——. *Sifat al-Safwah* (Beirut: Dar al-Kitab al-'Arabi, 2008).

Al-Jawziyyah, ibn Qayyim. *Jalaa al-Afham fi Fadl al-Salah wa al-Salam 'ala Muhammad Khayr al-Anam* (Riyadh: Dar al-Jawziyyah, 2010).

Al-Jazari, Shams al-Din. *Asma al-Manaqib fi Tadhhib Asna al-Matalib fi Manaqib al-Imam Amir al-Mu'minin Ali ibn Abi Talib* (Beirut: Dar al-Kutub al-'Ilmiyyah. 2005).

Al-Jiylani, Abd al-Qadir. *Al-Ghunyah li Talibi Tariq al-Haqq wa al-Din* (Beirut: Dar al-Khayr, 2005).

Al-Jiylani, Isma'il. *Al-Fuyudat al-Rabbaniyyah fi al-Maathir wa al-Awrad al-Qadiriyyah* (Damascus: Maktabah Dar al-Duqqaq, 2015).

Al-Jushami, al-Muhsin. *'Uyun al-Masa'il fi al-Usul* (Istanbul: Dar al-Ihsan, 2018).

Ibn Kathir, Isma'il. *Al-Bidayah wa al-Nihayah* (Beirut: Maktabah al-Ma'arif, 2016).

——. *Mukhtasar Tafsir ibn Kathir* (Beirut: Dar al-Qur'an al-Karim, 1973).

——. *The Life of the Prophet Muhammad* [al-Sira al-Nabawiyya], trans. Trevor Le Gassick (United Kingdom: Garnet Publishing, 2000).

Al-Kattani, Muhammad al-Baqir. *Rawqat al-Najjat fi Mawlid Khatim al-Risalat* (Beirut: Dar al-Kutub al-'Ilmiyyah, 2003).

Al-Kattani, Muhammad al-Nasir. *'Uyun al-Athar Fima Tawatur al-Ahadith*

wa al-Akhbar (Casablanca: Dar al-Hadith al-Kattaniyyah, 1996).

Al-Khadari, Abu al-Khayr. *Juz fi 'Adam Sihhah ma Nuqil 'an Bilal bin Rabah min Ibdalih al-Shin fi al-Adhan Sinan* (Beirut: Dar al-Basha'ir, 2002).

Al-Khalili, Muhammad. *Min Amali al-Imam al-Sadiq wa Huwa Sharh ma Umalah al-Imam 'ala Talmidhih al-Mufaddil bin 'Umar al-Ju'fi* (Beirut: Mu'assasah al-'Ala, 1984).

Al-Khawarizmi, Abu al-Mu'ayyid. *Maqtal al-Husayn* (Qom: Dar Anwar al-Huda, 1997).

Ibn Khuzaymah, Abu Bakr. *Kitab al-Tawhid wa Ithbat Siffat al-Rabb 'Azza wa Jall* (Riyadh: Dar al-Rushd, 2008).

Al-Kulayni, Muhammad. *Usul al-Kafi* (Tehran: Dar al-Kutub al-Islamiyyah, 1962).

Al-Kurdi, Yusuf. *Al-Intisar li al-Awliya al-Akhyar* (Beirut: Dar al-Kutub al-'Ilmiyyah, 2007).

Madelung, Wilferd. *Akhbar A'immah al-Zaydiyyah fi Tabaristan wa Dalaman wa Jiylan* (Beirut: Orient-Istitut der Deutschen Morgenlandischen Gesellschaft, 1987).

Ibn Majah, Abu Abdillah Muhammad ibn Yazid al-Qazwini. *Sunan ibn Majah* (Beirut: Darl al-Kutub al-'Ilmiyyah, 1998).

Ibn Majid, Abd al-Rahman. *Ansab al-Talibin wa al-'Alawiyyin al-Qadimiyyin wa Nabdhah min Akhbarihim* (Cairo: Wazarah al-Thaqafi, 2002).

Al-Majlisi, Muhammad. *Bihar al-Anwar al-Jami'ah li Dirar Akhbar al-A'immah al-Athar* (Beirut: Dar Ihya al-Turath al-'Arabi, 1983).

Ibn Manzur, Muhammad. *Lisan al-'Arab* (Beirut: Dar al-Sadir, 2010).

Al-Maqrizi, Taqi al-Din. *Kitab al-Mawa'iz wa al-'Itibar bi al-Khutt wa al-Athar li Ma'ruf bi al-Khutt li al-Maqrizi* (Beirut: Dar al-Kutub al-'Ilmiyyah, 1998).

Al-Mizzi, Yusuf. *Tahdhib al-Kamal fi Asma al-Rijal* (Beirut: Mu'assasah al-Risalah, 2008).

Al-Mu'ayyid, Ali. *Tathqif al-Ummah bi Sirah Awlad al-A'immah* (Beirut: Dar al-'Ilm, 2005).

Al-Mu'ayyidi, Majd al-Din. *Al-Masabih* (Amman: Mu'assasah al-Imam Zayd bin 'Ali al-Thaqafiyyah, 2002).

—. *Al-Tuhf Sharh al-Zalaf* (Sana'a: Mu'assasah Ahl al-Bayt, 1993).

Al-Mu'ayyidi, Muhammad. *Zubad al-Ad'iyyah*

(Sa'dah: Mu'assasah al-Mustafa al-Thaqafiyyah, 2003).

Mubarak, Ahmad, and Dawud Walid. *Centering Black Narrative: Ahl al-Bayt, Blackness & Africa* (Rockford: Itrah Press, 2019).

—. *Centering Black Narrative: Black Muslim Nobles Among the Early Pious Muslims* (Rockford: Itrah Press, 2016).

Ibn Muhammad al-Baqir, Ja'far al-Sadiq. *Misbah al-Shari'ah* (Beirut: Mu'assasah al-A'alami, 1992).

Ibn Musa al-Kazim, Ali al-Rida. *Sahifah al-Imam al-Rida* (Qom: Mu'assasah al-Imam al-Mahdi, 1987).

Al-Musawi, Ali. *Amali al-Murtada Ghurar al-Fawa'id wa Durar al-Qala'id* (Beirut: Maktabah al-'Asriyyah, 2009).

Al-Musawi, Mahdi. *Al-Mu'qibun min Aal Abi Talib* (Qom: Mu'assasah 'Ashura, 2016).

Muslim, ibn al-Hajjaj Abu al-Husayn. *Sahih Muslim* (Riyadh: Bayt al-Afkar al-Dawlah, 1998).

Al-Musuli, Abu Ya'la. *Musnad Abi Ya'la al-Musuli* (Beirut: Dar al-Kutub al-'Ilmiyyah, 1998).

Al-Nasa'i, Ahmad. *Khasa'is Amir al-Mu'minin 'Ali bin Abi Talib* (Beirut: Dar al-Kitab al-'Arabi, 1996)

—. *Sunan al-Nasa'i* (Beirut: Dar al-Kutub al-'Ilmiyyah, 2018).

Al-Nasiri, Ahmad. *Al-Maraqid al-Islamiyyah fi al-'Alam* (Beirut: Dar al-Hadi, 2006).

Nasrullah, Sa'd. *Dawlah al-Adarisah fi al-Maghrib al-'Asr al-Dhahabiyyah* (Beirut: Dar al-Nahdah al-'Arabiyyah, 1996).

Al-Nawawi, Abu Zakariya. *Al-Minhaj fi Sharh Sahih Muslim bin al-Hajjaj* (Beirut: Mu'assasah al-Risalah, 2015).

Al-Nu'man, Muhammad. *Al-Ikhtisas* (Najaf: Maktabah al-Saduq, 2009).

—. *Kitab al-Irshad* (Beirut: Mu'assasah al-A'alami, 2008).

Al-Qabbani, 'Adnan. *Al-Futuhat al-Haqqaniyyah fi Manaqib Ujula al-Silsilah al-Dhahabiyyah li al-Tariqah al-Naqshabandiyyah al-'Aliyyah* (Tripoli: Maktabah Ada bwa Fann, 2003).

Ibn al-Qasim, Ibrahim. *Tabaqat al-Zaydiyyah al-Kubra* (Amman: Mu'assasah al-Imam Zayd bin Ali al-Thaqafiyyah, 2001).

Qawuq, Nabil. *Hadha Huwa Bilal – Qira'ah fi Sirah al-Sahabi al-Jalil wa 'Alaqatih bi al-Nabi wa Ahl Baytih* (Beirut: Dar al-Mawaddah, 2016).

Al-Quda'i, Abu Abdullah. *Tarikh al-Quda'i* (Beruit: Dar al-Kutub al-'Ilmiyyah, 2004).

Ibn Qudamah, Muwwafaq al-Din. *Al-Mughni* (Riyadh: Dar al-'Alam al-Kutub, 1997).

Al-Qummi, Abbas. *Muntaha al-Amal fi Tawarikh al-Nabi wa al-Aal* (Beirut: Dar al-Mustafa al-'Alamiyyah, 2011).

Ibn Qutaybah, Abu Muhammad. *Al-Ma'arif* (Beirut: Dar al-Kutub al-'Ilmiyyah, 2011).

Al-Razi, Ahmad. *Akhbar Fakhkh wa Khabr Yahya bin Abdillah wa Akhih Idris bin Abdillah* (Tunis: Dar al-Gharb al-Islami, 2011).

Al-Razi, Fakhr al-Din. *Al-Shajarah al-Mubarakah fi Ansab al-Talibyyah* (Qom: Maktabah Ayatillah al-'Uzma al-Mar'ashi al-Najafi, 1998).

Al-Razi, Muhammad. *Mukhtar al-Sihah* (Beirut: Maktabah Libnan, 1989).

Al-Rifa'i, Ahmad. *Al-Rifa'i, Halah Ahl al-Haqiqah ma'a Allah Taa'la* (Beirut: Dar al-Kutub al-'Ilmiyyah, 2010).

Ibn Rustam, Abu Ja'far. *Dala'il al-A'immah* (Beirut: Mu'assasah al-'Ala, 1988).

Ibn al-Sabbagh, Ali. *Al-Fusul al-Muhimmah fi Ma'rifah Ahwal al-A'immah* (Beirut: Mu'assasah al-A'alami, 1988).

Ibn Sa'ad, Abu Abdullah. *Al-Tabaqat al-Kubra* (Cairo: Maktabah al-Khanaji, 2001).

Al-Safarini, Muhammad. *Al-Buhur al-Zakharah fi 'Ulum al-Akhirah* (Riyadh: Dar al-'Asimah, 2008).

Al-Sakhawi, Ali. *Tuhfah al-Ahbab wa Bughyah al-Tullab* (Cairo: Dar al-Muqattam, 2010).

Al-Salawi, Ahmad. *Al-Istiqsa li al-Akhbar Duwal al-Maghrib al-Aqsa* (Beirut: Dar al-Kutub al-'Ilmiyyah, 2018).

Al-Samarqandi, Husayn. *Tuhfah al-Talib bi Ma'rifah man Yantasib ila Abdillah wa Abi Talib* (Beirut: Mu'assasah Aal al-Bayt, 2011).

Al-San'ani, Muhammad. *Subul al-Salam Sharh Bulugh al-Maram min Adillah al-Ahkam* (Riyadh: Maktabah al-Ma'arif, 2006).

Al-Saqqaf, Hadi. *Al-Jawahar Al-Masun fi Rawayah Qalun* (Beirut: Dar al-Hawi, 1997).

Al-Saqqaf, Hasan. *Sahih Sharh al-Aqidah al-Tahawiyyah* (Cairo: Dar al-Imam al-Nawawi, 1995).

Al-Sayaghi, Husayn. *Al-Rawd al-Nadir Sharh Majmu'a al-Fiqh al-Kabir*

(Beirut: Dar al-Jiyl, 2005).

Al-Shablanji, Mu'min. *Nur al-Absar fi Manaqib Aal Bayt al-Nabi al-Mukhtar* (Beirut: Dar al-Kutub al-'Ilmiyyah, 2008).

Ibn Shahrashub, Abu Ja'far. *Manaqib Aal Abi Talib* (Beirut: Mu'assasah al-A'alami, 2009).

Al-Shahrudi, Ali. *Mustadrakat 'Ilm Rijal al-Hadith* (Tehran: Husayniyat 'Imad Zadah, 1992).

Ibn al-Shajari, Hibbatullah. *Amali bin al-Shajari* (Cairo: Dar al-Khanaji, 2014).

—. *Ma Ittafaq Lafzuhu wa Ikhtilaf Ma'nah* (Beirut: Dar al-Kutub al-'Ilmiyyah, 1996).

Shams al-Din, Muhammad. *Ansar al-Husayn: Darasah 'an Shuhada Thawrah al-Husayn al-Rijal wa al-Dalalat* (Beirut: Mu'assasah al-Dawliyyah, 1996).

Al-Sha'rani, Abd al-Wahab. *Al-Minan al-Kubra* (Beirut: Dar al-Kutub al-'Ilmiyyah, 2010).

—. *Al-Tabaqat al-Kubra* (Beirut: Dar al-Kutub al-'Ilmiyyah, 2018).

Al-Sha'rawi, Muhammad. *Ana min Sulalah Aal al-Bayt – al-Janib al-Ruh min Hayat al-Imam al-Sha'rawi* (Cairo: Dar al-Rawdah, 2013).

Al-Shinqiti, Muhammad al-Amin. *Adwa al-Bayan fi Idah al-Qur'an bi al-Qur'an* (Cairo: Al-Dar al-'Alamiyyah, 2014).

Sibt bin al-Jawzi, Yusuf bin Kizoghlu. *Tadhkirah al-Khawass* (Beirut: Dar al-Kutub al-'Ilmiyyah, 2005).

Al-Sijistani, Abu Dawud. *Al-Marasil ma'a al-Asanid* (Beirut: Dar al-Qalam, 1986).

—. *Sunan Abi Dawud* (Damascus: Al-Risalah al-'Alamiyyah, 2008).

Al-Suhrawardi, Umar. *Awarif al-Ma'arif* (Beirut: Dar al-Kutub al-'Ilmiyyah, 2016).

Al-Suyuti, Jalal al-Din. *Al-Hawi li al-Fatawa* (Beirut: Dar al-Kitab al-'Arabi, 2014).

—. *Kitab Raf' Sha'n al-Hubshan* (Beirut: Dar al-Kutub al-'Ilmiyyah, 2004).

—. *Sunan al-Nasa'i bi Sharh al-Suyuti wa Hashiyyahas-Sanadi* (Beirut: Dar al-Ma'rifah, 2008).

—. *Tarikh al-Khulafa* (Beirut: Dar al-Ma'rifah, 1997).

Al-Tabarani, Sulayman. *Al-Mu'jam al-Kabir* (Mosul: Matba'ah al-Zahra al-Hadithah, 1984).

—. *Al-Tafsir al-Kabir* (Amman: Dar al-Kitab al-Thaqafi, 2016).

Al-Tabari, Abu Ja'far. *Tahdhib al-Athar: Musnad Ali bin Abi Talib* (Cairo: Al-Mu'assasah al-Sa'udiyyah, 1982).

—. *Tafsir al-Tabari* (Beirut: Dar al-Kutub al-'Ilmiyyah, 1992).

—. *Tarikh al-Tabari* (Amman: Bayt al-Afkar, 2009).

Al-Tabarsi, Hasan. *Makarim al-Akhlaq* (Beirut: Mu'assasah al-A'alami, 2009).

Al-Tamimi, An-Nu'man. *Sharh al-Akhbar fi Fa'da'il al-A'immah al-Athar* (Qom: Mu'assasah an-Nashr al-Islami, 2016).

Ibn Taymiyyah, Taqi al-Din. *Majmu'a Fatawa Shaykh al-Islam bin Taymiyyah* (Beirut: Dar al-Kutub al-'Ilmiyyah, 2015).

Al-Tayyibi, 'Ukkashah. *Al-Jifr wa al-Fitan wa Ashrat al-Sa'ah* (Beirut: Dar al-Yusuf, 1999).

Al-Tha'labi, Ahmad. *Ahl al-Bayt fi Tafsir al-Tha'labi* (Qom: Markaz al-Buhuth wa al-Darasat Ma'ahd al-Qur'an al-Karim, 1962).

Al-Thamari, Ihsan, and Muhammad al-Qadhat. *Rasa'il min al-Turath al-Sufi fi Labs al-Khirqah* (Amman: Dar al-Razi, 2002).

Al-Tijani, Ahmad. *Al-Fayd al-Rabbani fi al-Tafsir wa al-Hadith* (Beirut: Dar al-Hadith al-Kattaniyyah, 2012).

Al-Tirmidhi, Abu 'Isa. *Sunan al-Tirmidhi* (Beirut: Dar al-Kutub al-'Ilmiyyah, 2017).

Al-'Ubaydi, Asiya. *Aal al-Bayt al-'Alawiyyah fi al-Maghrib wa Atharuhum fi al-Hayat al-'Ammah* (Beirut: Dar al-Kutub al-'Ilmiyyah, 2020).

Al-Wahidi, Ali ibn Ahmad. *Asbab al-Nuzul*, trans. Mokrane Guezzou (Amman: Royal Aal al-Bayt Institute for Islamic Thought, 2008).

Al-Waqidi, Abu Abdullah. *Futuh al-Sham* (Beirut: Dar al-Kutub al-'Ilmiyyah, 2005).

Al-Wasiti, Sharif al-Din. *Al-Burhan al-Mu'ayyid li Sahib Madd al-Yad Mawlana al-GhawtAl-Sharif al-Rifa'i Ahmad* (Beirut: Dar al-Kutub al-'Ilmiyyah, 2010).

Wehr, Hans. *Dictionary of Modern Written Arabic: Arabic-English. 4th Revised Edition*, ed. J. M. Cowan (Urbana, Illinois: Spoken Language Services Inc. U.S, 1994).

Ya'qub, Muhammad. *Al-Silsilah al-Dhahabiyyah fi Manaqib al-Sadah al-Naqshabandiyyah* (Damascus: Dar al-Farabi, 2004).

Al-Ya'qubi, Ahmad. *Tarikh al-Ya'qubi* (Beirut: Mu'assasah al-A'alami, 1993).

Al-Zamakhshari, Mahmud. *Al-Fa'iq fi Gharib al-Hadith* (Beirut: Dar al-'Asriyyah, 2011).

—. *Tafsir al-Kashshaf 'an Haqa'iq al-Tanzil wa 'Uyun al-Aqawil fi Wujuh al-Ta'wil* (Beirut: Dar al-Ma'rifah, 2005).

Zay'ur, Ali. *Kamil al-Tafsir al-Sufi al-'Irfani li al-Qur'an 'inda al-Sadiq* (Beirut: Maktabah al-Shawq, 2002).

Al-Zayn, Samih 'Atif. *Tafsir Mufradat Alfaz al-Qur'an al-Karim* (Beirut: Dar al-Kutub al-'Alami, 1994).

Al-Zubaydi, Murtada. *Al-Rawd al-Jalli fi Ansab Aal Ba'Alawi* (Damascus: Dar Kinan, 2010).

Al-Zu'bi, Abd al-Majid. *Ithaf al-Akabir fi Sirah wa Manaqib al-Imam Muhyi al-Din Abd al-Qadir al-Jiylani al-Hasani al-Husayni wa Ba'd Mashahir Dhurriyatih Uli al-Fadl wa Maathir* (Beirut: Dar al-Kutub al-'Ilmiyyah, 2007).

Unpublished Sources

Al-Jushami, al-Hakim. *Jalaa al-Absar* (Collection of Maktabah Jami' al-Kabir, Sana'a).

About Algorithm

> *Indeed, in the creation of the heavens and earth, and the alternation of the night and the day, and the [great] ships which sail through the sea with that which benefits people, and what Allah has sent down from the heavens of rain, giving life thereby to the earth after its lifelessness and dispersing therein every [kind of] moving creature, and [His] directing of the winds and the clouds controlled between the heaven and the earth are signs for a people who use reason.*
>
> (Q.2:164)

These verses have inspired innumerable scholars and philosophers to look to the heavens and the earth, nature and the cosmos for signs and patterns. Like Khawarizmi, who searched the universe for patterns, processes and rules that connected everything to one another, and ultimately connected us to our Creator. His quest led him to uncover the mysteries of algebra and algorithms.

Since then, humanity has made leaps and bounds in the fields of mathematics and science, in large part due to the discoveries of Khawarizmi. Today, we live in the age of algorithms, where they shape the world around us.

Whether it is our personal computers, data held by authorities or the oceans of material available on the internet, our world is ever increasingly reliant on algorithms for the sharing and understanding of data and information that allows for the smooth running of society.

Today, algorithms are used to sift through large amounts of information and their output can shape how businesses target customers, how banks approve loans, what news you see on your social media feed, and helps governments understand population trends as well as much, much more. Algorithms are shaping everything around us.

But few people think about the nature of the world that is being created by these algorithms. Few consider the ramifications of uploading their whole life onto social media. Little concern is paid to companies learning our habits and targeting us with material they know will keep us coming back, addicted to the virtual world they have created.

algorithm aims to publish works that we believe make a significant contribution to the religious, social and political ideas of the modern Muslim world. We hope to present ideas and information that will help us question the world we live in, and give us the intellectual tools to actively build healthy and vibrant societies, rather than letting others shape the world we live in. We hope to share ideas from thinkers of the past and present, from individuals who would be classified as Islamic as well as those who would not.

Our publications focus on the following areas:

• Works addressing the relationship between Islam and society.
• Works informing the development of responses to contemporary challenges facing Islam and Muslim religious, social and political thought in today's world.
• Works that promote fair interpersonal relationships and intercultural communication, social justice and healthy family dynamics as well as analyses and approaches to issues such as culture, politics, community and world society as they relate to Islam and Muslim societies as a majority or minority group.
• Proceedings of conferences and seminars dealing with the above topics

algorithm focuses on the philosophy of being and non-being and what it means to exist in a chaotic world. It seeks ways to move the world from a state of disorder to order and questions how to establish world justice through a systematic algorithm of truth.

We hope the present work furthers our objectives and is of benefit to the academic and scholarly communities as well as the wider Muslim readership.